CW00859478

THE LIFE OF A FAMILY

IN THE BRITISH COLONIES

1915 - 1930's

REBECCA CLAYTON

ISBN: 978-1-6847-1463-6 (sc)
ISBN: 978-1-6847-1465-0 (e)

Because of the dynamic nature of the Internet, any web addresses or links contained in this book may have changed since publication and may no longer be valid. The views expressed in this work are solely those of the author and do not necessarily reflect the views of the publisher, and the publisher hereby disclaims any responsibility for them.

Any people depicted in stock imagery provided by Getty Images are models, and such images are being used for illustrative purposes only. Certain stock imagery © Getty Images.

Lulu Publishing Services rev. date: 01/30/2020

PREFACE

L ife in a British Colony was good. Heavens it was good. From the Middle and Far East to tropical Africa where time virtually stood still. In the early 1900's countless families ventured out to the colonies, pioneering their way thousands of miles to unknown worlds on other continents and the dawning of a new life. This is a gut wrenching life story of such a family. Life, and all its problems was, contrary to popular belief, much the same in these colonies as it was in England, their motherland. It reveals how ephemeral life is; how a lifestyle, safe and secure, can disintegrate like a fleeting mortal wave rolling to shore. Be sure to cherish your life, your family, your circumstances.

This book is dedicated to my beloved mother, without her precious existence in my life and the stories she related to me, this story would not have been possible.

CHAPTER 1

July1915 Ootacamund, India. Dorothy was far from nervous. Why should she be? She'd travelled on her own through Russia, China and west again to India and she was looking forward to her life with Charles, an officer in the Indian Army. She had known him for three months but little did she know, she didn't know him at all.

Margaret looked at Dorothy. She was quite stunning, a beautiful woman with high cheekbones and full lips, meticulously painted with strawberry red lipstick, accentuating her deep blue eyes.

"Ready Dorothy?" quizzed Margaret whose husband was also an army officer.

"Well, yes, ready as I'll ever be!" Dorothy sounded confident as she stumped out her cigarette in a conch shell, usefully transformed into an ashtray. "Sounds like the car outside. Charles has arranged for Peter to pick us up."

Dorothy closed the windows and shutters in her small room. She had rented a room in a huge old colonial house and was to move into married quarters with Charles after their wedding ceremony. She had packed all of her earthly belongings into an old scuffed leather suitcase that had been her wardrobe through China and India.

She walked to the door and looked back at the smoky room. She stood for a moment and sighed. The car horn sounded outside.

"Come on Dorothy. We'll be late." Margaret sounded anxious.

Dorothy closed the door gently behind her. Her suitcase was heavy and her stiletto heels felt like stilts. Even her legs were feeling like jelly. Don't be mad, she thought to herself. You're getting married to an officer in the army and life can only be wonderful from now on but she hesitated momentarily. Was her sixth sense telling her something else, she thought.

"Thank you Pete." Peter rushed towards Dorothy and took her suitcase from her. "I hope you haven't forgotten yesterdays rehearsal!" Dorothy was out of breath. "You've been a great friend to Charles and we're so grateful to you for agreeing to give me away. My poor father died last year and I know he would have been delighted to have done the honours today."

"I've known Charles for a few years now. I'm really happy for him today. He needs a woman to control him …" Peter stopped short and hurriedly put the suitcase in the boot of the car.

Dorothy thought his comment strange. "What do you mean 'control him'?"

"Oh, ah, nothing really!" Peter tried to make light of Dorothy's forceful questioning.

They drove through narrow streets, twisting and turning through the village and as they turned the last corner the little stone-clad church came into view. It was a pretty little building set amongst leafy trees and neatly manicured lawns.

"We're bang on time." Dorothy sounded confident again. "Maggie, you had better go in before us. Thanks for your help and support."

The church was packed. Charles and Dorothy had agreed on thirty guests and there must have been sixty there. The service was uneventful and they headed to a popular hotel outside the village for the reception. What a reception. It was bigger than Dorothy had anticipated. Charles had ordered the finest French champagne and there were crates and crates of it.

Dorothy nudged Charles. "Charles darling, this is going to cost a fortune!"

"Don't worry my sweet. You're the best thing that's happened in my life and I want to make sure you have nothing but the best."

The champagne and wine flowed freely late into the night and Dorothy was relieved when the guests started to thin out. Her feet were aching. It was shortly before midnight when Charles and Dorothy bid farewell to the last of their guests. Charles had booked the honeymoon suite in the hotel and they gladly headed for their room.

"Thank you my darling. You made me feel like a queen." Dorothy was feeling light headed but was not inebriated enough not to be aware of her sexual feelings.

Charles sat on the bed and took off his shoes. "That was the whole idea. You *are* my queen, the light of my life."

Dorothy and Charles prepared to go to dinner on their second night. She sat on the dressing table stool, richly covered in gold and blue embossed velvet. She looked at Charles through the mirror as she had a long drink from her beer glass. She placed the glass down gently on the dressing table and continued to screw on her earrings. Charles was ready and was leaning against the windowsill, beer glass in hand.

"Are you ready, my darling?" asked Charles in a relaxed tone.

"I'm almost there." Dorothy had stretched her upper lip to apply her red lipstick, making her voice sound aristocratic. And so it should have. Dorothy was born in England in 1886 to a wealthy family. She had a good education, was well read, an accomplished pianist and singer, and spoke eloquently. In her early twenties she had an arranged marriage to a Belgium Baron in Paris. He was much older than her but died from pneumonia several months after their marriage.

After she was widowed she booked to go on the Titanic's maiden voyage to America in 1912. Fate would not allow her journey on the doomed ship because she changed her mind and in great pioneering spirit headed east on the Trans Siberian Railway to Shanghai. From there she travelled to Canton, then to India where she met Charles, an officer with the Royal Engineers in the British Army. She was a wealthy woman in her own right having inherited her father's estate and the stately fortune from her elderly deceased Baron.

She was a fine woman, dressed immaculately and carried herself well. She certainly *looked* wealthy and although she and Charles had only known each other for three months, they never discussed her financial status.

Dorothy's earrings were in place and she struggled to fasten the matching necklace around her neck. She didn't have to ask Charles to help her.

"I'm starving. I wonder what's on the menu tonight. Shall we wander down to the sitting room?" Charles quizzed her through the mirror.

The passages were wide with high pressed ceilings. Continuous lengths of red and gold carpets adorned the wooden strip floorboards throughout the hotel and leafy tropical pot plants in heavy brass containers crowded the corridors, landings and foyer.

Couples were sparsely seated in the main sitting room and

although the atmosphere was humid, a breeze flowed through the French doors opening onto the veranda cooling the air with the assistance of over-head fans flying around at hurricane speed. Dorothy and Charles ordered their Scotch and soda and sat alone in low back red leather chairs, the smell of leather permeating the room.

"Cheers," their crystal glasses clicked together and they sipped the pure spirit. Warmed with the intake of their drinks they went into the dining room and dined like royalty but Dorothy felt unsettled, something wasn't right.

"Let's go on the veranda and cool off." Charles led her outside after dinner.

The hotel was the ideal retreat for a honeymoon, a typical colonial building built specifically for warmer climates with wide verandas that overlooked sweeping green lawns, dotted with fishponds and secluded waterfalls flowing gently over granite rocks. The gardens were particularly attractive in the evenings with strategic lights illuminating the waterfalls, lawns and palm trees. Charles and Dorothy sat arm in arm and took in the scenery, the sound of chirping crickets adding to the tranquillity of the night. Dorothy was anxious, concerned at the cost of their stay. It was a top class hotel and Charles was sparing nothing. He was an army officer yes, but heavens, could his salary cope with such extravagance? She sighed and snuggled down into his chest.

"How about a liqueur?" asked Charles.

"Yes, why not!" said Dorothy as she slid a cigarette into her lengthy cigarette holder.

Charles waved to a nearby waiter. "Can we have two liqueurs please?"

"Certainly sir." The waiter hurried away.

Dorothy blew her cigarette smoke high into the air. "Charles, will you be able to afford our stay here? I'm sure it's going to cost you a fortune."

"Well, yes, I'm sure it won't be that much. Don't you worry about that." Charles didn't sound concerned.

Dorothy sat on the veranda of her new home with a cup of tea in one hand and a cigarette in the other. Although it was 4 o'clock in the afternoon the sun was hot. It felt good and she was as brown as a berry. They had been in the officers married quarters for two months and life was being kind to them. Charles had a batman, Jay, who as an angel. He managed to do so much in a day and was always willing and cheerful. He brought them their early morning tea, prepared breakfast, did the laundry. Ironing Charles' uniform each day seemed so easy for him. The tunics were heavily starched and required ironed without a single crease but somehow he managed. Then there were the other bits and pieces to go with the uniform. The brass buttons, brass badges of rank not to mention the brass buckles on the leather belt and Sam brown. Spit and polish were the order of the day.

Dorothy sat with her eyes shut and heard the familiar scuffle of bare feet. It was Jay.

"Excuse me Mrs Butler. Will you and Mr Butler need anything for dinner?" Dorothy more often than not prepared dinner, usually a light snack, but Jay was always willing to go that extra mile.

"No thank you Jay. Mr Butler should be home in about an hour. I'll prepare dinner."

Jay gave a slight bow turned on his heels and disappeared quickly into the house.

Dorothy lit another cigarette and sighed. Charles had been arriving home late some nights and he assured her he had been catching up on paperwork in the office. It was becoming more regular now. At first it was 9 or 10 o'clock and some nights it was nearly midnight when he'd slink quietly into the house.

She put her cigarette out in a delicately designed pewter ashtray and went into the house. She was happy there but something kept nagging her. She remembered Peter's comments when he took her to the church on her wedding day… '"He needs a woman to control him."' She kept telling herself not to be concerned about it but it kept coming back to haunt her. What did Pete mean? Dorothy was tempted to speak to Peter but pride prevented it.

7 o'clock. Not another late night she thought. It seemed to be heading that way. Charles smelt of whisky when he returned from his previous late night out. She pondered as she prepared herself a sandwich in the kitchen. I'm not a fool or a walkover she thought to herself. Why didn't I quiz him that night? He said he'd been at the office yet he smelt of liquor. He wasn't drunk by any means. He was his usual polite, cheerful self. Surely there's not another woman? She'd walk out and kill him. Well, not in that order. She'd kill him first then walk out. She wasn't going to put up with that carry on. Forget it.

She turned on the radio and it crackled into life. Someone was blurting out a news bulletin from London. Very boring she thought. She paced the huge kitchen. Oh heavens, what am I going to do? Her mind was still racing. She wanted to speak to Peter there and then. He lived in the single quarters only a twenty-minute walk away. No. She and Charles had to sort this out themselves without bringing the whole of the barracks into their private life.

It was quarter to twelve and Dorothy had elected to stay up. On previous nights when he had come home late she was in bed and to avoid any disagreements or arguments she had pretended to be asleep. She wanted some answers tonight.

Dorothy was sitting at the head of the oak dining table playing patience, her favourite card game. Patience in more than one way she often thought. She heard a car pull up at the front door. The engine stopped. Silence for a minute and the car door shut. The front door closed. She stared at the door into the sitting room anticipating Charles' appearance.

The dining room light was usually off and Charles sensed Dorothy's presence in the room. He walked slowly to the open door and stopped, Dorothy in his sight.

"Hello." He was nervous. "I'm so sorry I'm late again my darling. Work is just piling up. I'm really letting you down and we're not spending enough time together."

Dorothy had been ready to start the inquisition but suddenly she felt sorry for him. Was he *really* being honest, was he really working late? She'd let things slide this time, but not again.

"I'd like to make this up to you. Can I take you to dinner at the officer's mess tomorrow night?"

Dorothy couldn't bring herself to quiz him, not now. Anyway it was late and she was tired. "Yes my love. That would be great." She held out her hands to him and he walked over to her.

They walked up the steps to the officer's mess. There was a buzz inside. The doorman greeted them and showed them into the sitting room. There was a smell of cigarette and cigar smoke in the large room but that was overpowered by the strong smell of leather from the chairs. Eight ceiling fans spun around fervently as though wilful and determined to clear the smoke from the room. It was cosy and very plush.

Charles led Dorothy to a vacant table near one of the doors leading to the veranda. She sat down and he went to the bar to order their long cold beers, their thirst quenchers in the hot steamy Indian climate. They weren't alone for long when Charles' officer commanding, Sir Edmund Dalhousie and his wife Lady Mary, greeted them and Charles invited them to join their table. He was wondering if he had done the right thing but he had no choice.

"You met wife Dorothy as I recall, a few months ago?" Charles introduced Dorothy.

"Yes of course my dear." Sir Edmund kissed Dorothy's hand and gave her a naughty wink. "It's a pleasure to see you again."

Lady Mary fanned her face with a highly decorated Japanese fan and appeared unconcerned and accustomed to her husband's antics.

"Hello my dear. I trust you're settling in to married life?" Lady Mary sounded genuine. She was known for her sincerity and was always busily involved in charity work with the community.

"Yes. Thank you." Dorothy gave a nervous laugh. It was not the sort of evening Dorothy and Charles had envisaged.

Dorothy saw a couple sitting a short distance away and observed a woman waving in their direction. She saw Charles wave back and he smiled at the woman.

"Who's that?" whispered Dorothy.

Charles was blushing. "Oh just an old friend. Can I get you a drink Sir Edmund, Lady Mary?"

Dorothy was annoyed at Charles fobbing her off. He walked over to the bar and the mystery woman held out her hand and stopped him. Charles kissed the back of her hand, mimicking Sir Edmund's trick. Dorothy couldn't hear what they were saying but Charles only stopped momentarily to talk to her.

Sir Edmund lent back in the wide leather chair. He was a big man, over six feet tall and a big build. He had a ruddy, rugged face. "Tell me Dorothy. What have you been doing since moving into the officers married quarters? I trust you've found plenty to do?"

"Well, actually." Dorothy hesitated, and then thought to hell with it. She remembered she had a mind of her own. "Charles has been working late on and off for a number of weeks and we haven't been able to plan many outings."

"Oh. Hmm." Sir Edmund looked blankly into the room. He looked puzzled and rubbed his chin. "I'm not aware of any staff working excessively late. I'll have to look..."

"Here we are." Charles guided the waiter to their table.

Dorothy was agitated. She hated uncertainty. Blast it she thought. Damn, damn, damn.

They had a superb meal and sat with the Dalhousies. The Scotch flowed freely and the evening went without a hitch. All four were ticking nicely when they bade their farewells well after midnight.

Charles' driver was waiting for them outside the mess and drove them home. Dorothy felt warm and contented and she wasn't thinking about Sir Edmunds comments earlier in the evening.

Two nights had passed. It was 10.30 in the evening and Dorothy was alone. It's happening again, she thought.

"Damn it." she said out loud to herself.

Her thoughts were muddled. Who *was* that woman waving at Charles? Sir Edmund said staff weren't working late. So what the hell was Charles up to? She was fed up. Married for nearly three months and now this. She had to get a straight answer from Charles. She sat in the sitting room gazing into space thinking about that trip she never took on the Titanic and it's ultimate demise into the bowels of the dark cold Atlantic. She was glad of her decision. After all, she'd never have met Charles. She loved him dearly and she knew in her heart of hearts that he cherished her. But just what was he up to? She was miles away when she heard Charles' voice.

"Hello darling."

"Good grief, you gave me a fright. These late nights are really becoming a habit Charles. I think we'd better talk this over as two responsible adults." Dorothy sounded sincere. She found it difficult to sound or feel angry. She wasn't going to leave anything to chance. "Sir Edmund told me the other evening that staff weren't working late, yet you've be telling me you've been working late at the office. What am I to believe?"

Charles took his hands out of his pockets. He thought that looked confrontational and he certainly didn't feel like that inside. "My love, my love, what can I say." He hung his head and walked over to the mantelpiece, his back to Dorothy. He couldn't face her.

Dorothy was almost nervous. What was he going to say?

"The truth is." He stopped and placed both hands on the mantelpiece, looking down at his feet. "Dorothy, I'm in debt. Up to my bloody neck in it." He'd said it. He knew she'd have to know eventually but not this soon into their marriage.

"So? What has that to do with your supposedly 'late nights at the office'?" She sounded almost sarcastic but she wanted the truth.

"I, I um. I've been meeting with some of the chaps in the Sergeant's Mess." He knew he was getting nowhere but found it hard to be straight with Dorothy.

Dorothy sat on the couch. She didn't move or say anything.

Charles was hoping for a prompt from her but it wasn't forthcoming. He felt very uncomfortable. His throat was dry. He walked over to the bar in the corner of the room, still with his back to Dorothy. "Scotch?"

"Yes please." Dorothy wasn't helping him and offered no comment.

He poured two drinks and turned to face Dorothy. She was looking straight at him and had a blank look on her face. He wasn't sure how to read into that. He sighed and walked over to her, handed her a glass and sat down at the far end of the couch.

"I've been gambling. I'm trying to sort out my finances and I hoped that playing poker would solve my problems. It just isn't working and I'm getting deeper and deeper in the crap, to put it bluntly." He sat on the edge of the couch rolling his glass in his hands.

"What do you owe and to who?" Dorothy wasn't convinced.

"Oh I don't know. It's all just piling up."

"For heavens sake Charles, you must know how much you owe your creditors and who are they? This is crazy. You'll have to be straight with me, you know that. If our marriage is going to stay intact we can only be honest with each other. There's no other way."

Charles knew she was right. "I love you more than you'll ever know and I want you to have the very best and I'll go to any length to see that you have the best."

"Don't tell me you've been frequenting the Sergeants Mess. A Major and an engineer at that, and you have to play poker in the Sergeants Mess. For goodness sake Charles. I bet you Peter is a partner in this too, is he?" Dorothy seemed more concerned about his reputation.

"Well, yes, as a matter of fact Pete is one of the regular four. It's very much a closed shop." Charles felt deflated. He had let down the woman who meant everything to him. "I'm so, so sorry my love. You know what you mean to me and hurting you is the last thing in the world I would want to do."

"How much do you owe?"

Charles didn't answer straight away. He walked over to the window. The lights were not bright on the veranda but they threw a delicate light onto the lawn and date trees in the garden. It looked neat, crisp and green. He needed confidence to continue. He swirled the last bit of whisky in his glass and the crystal tinkled from the ice. He knocked it back and poured himself another Scotch. He poured another for Dorothy and went back to the window. He couldn't face her. He took a deep breath. "Too much. Too damn much."

"How much is 'too much'?" She sounded impartial.

"Four, five thousand pounds". He knew it had to come out eventually.

"That's a lot of money in any man's language. Why in heavens name do you owe so much?"

"Dorothy, I'm an impulsive gambler. I've been gambling for years. I've managed to keep my head above water all these years but things are getting on top of me. I've been borrowing to gamble to pay off the debts and the whole thing is out of control. I owe money to bookies in London as well." He felt like a fool but his problem wasn't new, well not new to him and he wondered how she would react to it.

An 'impulsive gambler.' The words stuck in Dorothy's mind. Surely not, she thought. All of a sudden her wealth felt important to her. Neither of them had discussed finances before. It seemed irrelevant. Money was never important to Dorothy and she presumed Charles felt the same way. Her mind was racing. She didn't want to be dishonest with Charles. No. She needn't be. Not disclosing her wealth is not being 'dishonest' she thought. She's just not telling him. No harm in that.

"Your salary must be a pittance compared to what you owe. You'll never be able to settle that."

"I don't want you to worry about that my love. I'm sure I'll be able to settle it in a few months."

"And how do you propose doing that? Gamble I suppose?"

"I've got myself out of debt before and I'll do it again. I just need a few good hands at poker and I'll be fine." Charles sounded confident, as gamblers usually do.

"No Charles. That's not the answer. You're going to get yourself deeper and deeper into the mire." She wanted to help him. She loved him passionately but she wanted to be careful how she handled it. She was afraid that if he knew her wealth his gambling would continue.

"I have a little money in England, a small inheritance from my father. Let's settle your debts and start afresh. But please Charles, I want you to promise me, promise me faithfully, you'll stop this obsession."

Charles felt terrible but at the same time he knew he was up to his neck in debt and getting out of it this time was going to be hard, if not impossible. "How can I allow you to do that? It's not right. Shall we sleep on it?"

"I don't think we have a choice. If you owe that money, it should be paid and gambling is not going to solve the problem." Dorothy was a level headed woman. "Give me details of what's owed to who and let's get this behind us. Come on, it's late. Let's get to bed."

CHAPTER 2

K andi, Ceylon, 1921. Dorothy was heavily pregnant with their second child. Betty, now two, was born in England. Dorothy's life had had so many ups and downs, highs and lows over the last six years that she knew exactly what it was like to be in heaven and the pits of hell. She'd been in both places many times. Her social life had been great but her hardships with Charles had caused her great anguish and mental torment.

Charles' gambling had continued in Ceylon and Dorothy spent many a lonely night in their enormous rambling home in Kandi. Charles was earning a very good salary. He was an engineer by profession and had been seconded into the army during the war. He attested at the rank of Major and was well respected in his profession. The army was in need of professionals after the war and he elected to remain in the army.

His gambling was his downfall. Charles and Dorothy discussed it many times and he always promised to stop. It was like asking him to stop breathing. It was an obsession with him. Every six months or so, she would have to wire her bank in England so she could settle Charles' debts. It was an endless nightmare and the amounts increased. Dorothy couldn't fathom out if Charles was taking advantage of her bailing him out each time or if his problem was seriously getting worse. She feared it was the latter.

She knew Charles loved her and always showed his deepest regrets. His continual habit was seemingly beyond his control and he was taking Dorothy's goodwill for granted. She hadn't used her wealth to finance their living as she was, understandably, terrified that Charles would blow that too. His heart was in the right place and he never queried her financial status. He felt too proud. He wanted to give Dorothy the best of everything and his salary would have seen them through very nicely but his ghastly obsession only put them deeper and deeper in debt.

It was February and Dorothy was expecting her second baby in May. Although they now had a maid and their faithful batman Jay, who came with them when Charles was transferred from India to Ceylon, Dorothy liked to keep busy in the house. She was cutting flowers in the garden as Sir Edmund and Lady Mary were coming for dinner. It was his annual visit to Ceylon and he was to inspect the headquarters and barracks and address the troops. She liked them both and had corresponded with them on a regular basis. She had never mentioned Charles' problem to Sir Edmund and she often wondered if he was aware of it.

As Dorothy pondered, she saw Jay standing on the steps. "Excuse me Mrs Butler. What time will you be eating tonight?"

"Oh. Sir Edmund's arriving at 7.30, so I think 8.30 will be fine, thank you Jay."

Dorothy had cut the flowers just in time. The sky was black in the east and the clouds looked threatening. "We're in for a storm Jay. Could you ask Girlie to close the windows?" Girlie was their maid. Dorothy loved her and she was a gem with Betty. She was a local Indian in her late teens, a strong energetic woman with a round face, which was never without a smile. Her real name was Joyce. Her mother had worked for an English family and her mother chose the name after her employer. She was nicknamed 'Girlie' when she was a baby and the name stuck.

A few large drops of rain fell on Dorothy's arm and the black clouds lit up. About five seconds later there was a clap of thunder and she knew the storm wasn't far away. Many a time she had sat on the veranda alone on summer evenings and watched the storms. She knew so many seconds between the flash of lightning and the sound of thunder meant the storm was that many miles away. Betty clung to Dorothy's skirt. "Come on darling. Let's get inside." Betty ran up the wide wooden steps and Dorothy followed slowly, suddenly aware of the weight she was carrying in her belly.

As Dorothy walked through the hallway she could smell the roast lamb. Good, Jay had started cooking she thought as she went through to the kitchen. She found Girlie peeling the potatoes.

"I think fresh peas and pumpkin would be a nice combination, don't you think Girlie? Don't forget the mint sauce!"

Dorothy got two vases from the cupboard and prepared the flowers on a spare wooden table in the middle of the kitchen.

The darkness set in early that evening, the gaps between the lightning and thunder shortened until a huge crack of thunder shook the house as a flash of lightning lit up the garden and the lights flickered.

"That's all we need tonight." Dorothy spoke to herself.

"It'll probably snow tonight." She heard Charles' voice right behind her. He kissed her on her head.

Dorothy noted his sarcasm. "Yes indeed. If you're home so early tonight, it *will* snow! I presumed you'd be home early tonight anyway. Have a good day?"

The raindrops on the roof became more frequent and seconds

later the heavens opened and sounded like an orchestra in full swing, the tin roof accentuating the powerful crescendo. Thunder cracked right over the house again and a lightning flash lit the garden.

Charles had followed Dorothy into the dining room. She wanted to help Girlie lay the table but most if it had been done. Poor Girlie always muddled up the soup and dessertspoons and Dorothy walked around the table moving them into their correct places when she suddenly pulled out a chair and sat down. "Heavens, I feel dizzy."

"You've had a few turns like this recently darling. I think we should call the doctor." Charles sounded very concerned.

"Oh, it's nothing Charles. I'm pregnant. Remember?"

Charles walked up to her and held her head in his hands. "You look very pale. In fact you look a bit *yellow* and pale."

"Don't fuss my darling, I'll be fine. Now let's get ready. Our guests will be here shortly."

"Well even if I say so myself, Jay has excelled himself." Charles concealed a burp in his starched napkin. "Excuse me. Now who's for seconds? Lady Mary?"

"Those roast spuds were beautiful. I won't say no to another one. I'll have to play an extra game of tennis next week!"

Dorothy rang the little bell on the table to summons Girlie. "Sir Edmund?"

"No. No thank you. That was most enjoyable. I'm as full as a pig." Sir Edmund patted his stomach, which was surprisingly flat and muscular for a man of his age and stature.

"Would the ladies like a Port?" Charles walked over to the bar at the end of the dining room.

"I'd love coffee. Shall we have a chat in the sitting room Dorothy and leave these two hunks to enjoy their Port together?" Lady Mary had had a good few glasses of wine and she had to steady herself for a moment when she stood up from the table. "Woo, I've had one too many!" Lady Mary giggled, her speech slightly slurred.

Sir Edmund looked sternly at her over his spectacles. They glanced momentarily at each other and Lady Mary gave him a little wave. His authoritarian look dissolved and broke into a huge grin. "See you in a while. Have yourself a black coffee darling."

There were four coffee cups on the silver tray in the sitting room, Girlie wisely leaving nothing to chance. Dorothy poured their coffee and she sat gingerly in a leather chair.

Charles poured himself and Sir Edmund another Port.

"Charles, I've been hearing various reports over the last year about your..." Sir Edmund stopped. Charles was a personal friend and he hated doing this. But it was his duty, not only to the army but the Empire. Sir Edmund took a deep breath. "Let me get to the point Charles. Your obsession with gambling has people talking in high places in London. I had a wire from the Foreign Office last week asking me to approach you. In a nutshell Charles, you are an embarrassment to the Empire and the army and the whole bloody thing is falling on my shoulders as your commanding officer."

Charles was standing with his hand in one pocket and clutching his glass with the other. He turned to face Sir Edmund and looked down, staring at his feet.

"Damn and blast it. What the hell has London got to do with my personal life? I run a tight ship here Edmund and as you know I take my rank and profession very seriously. What I do in my own time has bugger-all to do with bloody London." Charles was decidedly agitated that his 'cover' had been blown. He thought only he and Dorothy were aware of his obsession.

"I know how you feel Charles. Gambling, when it controls your life, is an illness. It's like alcoholism. Alcoholics drink secretly and clearly you wanted your gambling to remain a secret. The thing…" Sir Edmund was stopped by another outburst from Charles.

"Don't bloody well lecture me. I know what I'm doing damn it."

"You've lost control. My office has several final demands from individuals andcompanies you've borrowed from in London. I'm talking to you as a friend Charles. If this doesn't stop, you'll be kicked out of the bloody army, to put it bluntly. And the boot will come from London. I'll have no control over it. I also understand engineers are needed in Hong Kong. That's between you and me, nothing official." Sir Edmund hesitated. "Heaven knows what you'd get up to there."

Charles was picking the dried wax from the side of a candle on the table. He stared blankly at the candle and only offered a quiet "Hmmm."

They were jolted out of an atmosphere neither were enjoying by Lady Mary shouting from the dining room door. "Edmund, Charles. Dorothy's collapsed. I think she's fainted. I think you should call the doctor."

Charles ran into the sitting room and found Dorothy on the floor, lying in the prone position. He felt her carotid artery. Her pulse was there but weak.

Engineer or no engineer, all army personnel had to learn basic first aid and although he'd never had to use it, his training came in useful.

"I've called Colonel Branch. He'll be here in a few minutes." Sir Edmund knelt down with Charles and they tried to rouse Dorothy.

"I hope she didn't fall on her stomach?" Charles looked worryingly at Lady Mary.

"No Charles. She tried to stand up but fell on her knees and onto her side. I'm quite sure there was no injury to the baby."

Dorothy started to murmur, opened her eyes and placed her hand on her forehead.

"I've got a dreadful headache. What happened?"

"You fainted my sweet. We've called the doctor." Charles placed a cushion under her head. "You were out for a few minutes. Now don't worry."

"You're the one worrying my darling."

"Hello? Can I come in?" Colonel Branch was at the door.

"Yes. Thank you Colonel." Sir Edmund beckoned him in to the room. "The Major's wife fainted and we thought you'd better have a look at her."

Colonel Branch was very tall and thin and wore half rimmed glasses on the end of his nose. His appearance lived up to his nickname 'Twiggy.'

He knelt down next to Dorothy and opened his brown leather bag. He put his stethoscope on her extended belly and listened intently for some time.

"The baby's fine. Now, how are you!" he exclaimed, trying to make light of a tense atmosphere. He placed a thermometer in her mouth and carried on using his stethoscope, listening to Dorothy's chest.

"You're a little yellow." He felt around her liver for some time.

"Yes doctor, I thought that earlier today when she had a dizzy spell and she tried to shrug it off with her pregnancy. What do you think it is?" Charles was still kneeling next to Dorothy.

"Hmm. 102.2. You've got a fever. I'd like to say it's malaria but I'm concerned about your colour. I'll need some blood samples and I'll carry out a few tests. I think we should get you to bed. You must rest. The baby's due in a few months. Now, are you feeling steady enough to stand?" The Colonel was taking control of the situation.

Dorothy managed the long walk down the passage to their bedroom with Charles and the Colonel on either side of her. She walked well but they wanted to be sure she didn't pass out again.

"Let me see Sir Edmund and Lady Mary off. I'm sure they're keen to get away now. I'll be back in a moment doctor." Charles hurried out of the room.

"What's wrong with me doctor? You know I'm fit and strong and I perish the thought of being under the weather. What is it?"

"We'll have a better understanding after I've carried out some blood tests. Now don't worry your pretty little head. I'll take the blood now and give you something to help bring down the fever and help you to sleep. I want you to stay in bed tomorrow."

"I can't stay in bed! I'm just not the type to linger. Ouch, that's a huge needle." She sounded frustrated and annoyed.

"I'll see you in the morning. Just relax and get some sleep." The tall thin slab hurried out of the room and Dorothy heard him talking to Charles in the passage.

It was nearly two months since Twiggy Branch told Dorothy and Charles the news. Dorothy had black water fever. It was thought to be akin to malaria but it affected and enlarged the liver hence the jaundice type symptoms she was experiencing. She continued to have attacks of biliousness and fever. Twiggy visited the house two or three times a week and was concerned about Dorothy's pregnancy.

Dorothy sat on the veranda in the late afternoon sun. The sun was still hot although it was now April and she only had her legs exposed to the sun. She was annoyed that she had no energy. She felt tired although she had done little in the last few months. Colonel Branch's words kept preying on her. 'I must let you know that foetal retardation often occurs in cases of black water fever.' She couldn't get those two words out of her mind. 'Foetal retardation.' It was like a nightmare coming back to haunt her everyday.

Charles had been a tower of strength. He was home straight after work most afternoons. They played chess when Dorothy was up to it or he sat in the chair in the bedroom on her bad days. Her 'bad days' were becoming more frequent and she was often bedridden with fever.

Charles drove slowly up the driveway and parked in front of the house. He saw Dorothy on the veranda and was relieved that she felt well enough to be up. He bundled a newspaper under his arm, pulled his heavy briefcase from the passenger seat and slammed the car door. He stood there and looked up at Dorothy.

"Hello darling." He put his paraphernalia at the top of the steps. "You worry me and I think about you every minute of the day. I spoke to Twiggy today and I suggested you go to London and have the baby there. He was adamant the treatment you're getting here is as good and up to date as it would be in England. How do you feel about it?"

"You know that would cost a small fortune. You really are the last of the big spenders Charles. In any event, I have every confidence in Colonel Branch. Black water fever is a bastard to get rid of and being here or in England wouldn't make the slightest difference. I'm just concerned about the baby but he tells me the heartbeat is strong. You're like a mother hen Charles. I love you for it but please stop worrying. I'll be fine. Thank you Jay." Jay had heard the car arriving and brought them a tray of tea and freshly made sandwiches.

They had had a quiet evening and went to bed early. Charles was a light sleeper and was woken at 4 o'clock with the sound of Dorothy groaning.

"What is it Dorothy?"

"I feel awful. I feel nauseous and my head's spinning. It's terribly hot. Can you put the fan on?" Dorothy's shortly cropped permed hair was saturated with perspiration.

"You've got a fever again. I'm calling the doctor." Charles ran into the hallway wearing only his pyjama shorts.

It was 2am and Dorothy was lying on her back, her torso propped up with half a dozen pillows. Her complexion was decidedly yellow against the crisp white starched sheets. She was in a private room in the local Government hospital in Kandi where all Officers and their families were automatically upgraded to private patient status. Her breathing was shallow and she had been in a semi-conscious state.

Charles was slumped in an armchair next to her bed. He cherished his beloved and was devastated by her illness. She meant everything to him and consequently had been at her bedside for three days since her admission. He would leave for the office at 7.30 each morning and was back at her side before 6 o'clock in evening having showered at home and changed into mufti. Good old Jay routinely placed a freshly ironed uniform in Charles' car. He ate his meals at the Officers Mess. Girlie, their maid and Betty's nanny had been a rock. She and Betty got on like a house on fire and during this upheaval she slept in the spare room in the house, right next to Betty's bedroom.

Charles hadn't slept well for the last few nights, waking frequently to check on Dorothy. Tonight he was extra tired, his head resting on the back of the chair with his mouth open and his raucous snoring was enough to put a herd of elephants to shame. The nightlight on the wall next to Dorothy's bed woke Charles, coupled with confusion in the room.

He had been in such a deep sleep he had been oblivious to Dorothy's screaming. Two nurses were calming her as she tried to get out of the bed. The drip stand supplying saline to Dorothy's arm was lying on the floor.

"Get it out of here. Get that bloody thing out of here. I hate them. Charles." Dorothy was shrieking at the top of her voice. "Charles, help me. Please please kill that thing. They're all over the room now. Charles." Dorothy was screaming and covering her face.

The nurses were having difficulty constraining her. Charles shook Dorothy lightly.

"What is it? What's the matter?"

"Those huge spiders. Look on the wall. Kill them Charles. Quickly."

"Dorothy darling. Listen to me. There are NO spiders in here. I promise. There are none. Believe me. You have been delirious for a few days. It's your fever and you 're hallucinating. Believe me darling. There is nothing there. Just lie back and shut your eyes." Charles had to alleviate her fears. She was arachnophobic at the best of times and living in India and Ceylon always posed a real threat of encountering those eight-legged hairy creatures.

The senior night Sister came into the room with a tray covered with a green cloth. She held a small syringe up to the dim light and pushed the plunger with her thumb, expelling the air until a clear liquid squirted momentarily onto the floor. One nurse rolled Dorothy onto her side and in a flash the Sister had inflicted the minute puncture in her rump.

"It's just a mild sedative to calm you down. High fevers can cause hallucinations. Can you see anything on the walls now?"

Dorothy closed her eyes and didn't answer. The nurses had picked up the drip stand and the Sister inserted a fresh needle into the back of Dorothy's hand and checked the saline bag hanging on the stand. It was half empty and she adjusted the drip flow and watched it for a few seconds.

"Everything should be all right now sir. Please push the bell if there are any problems but I'm quite sure she'll sleep now." The Sister and her entourage left the room.

"Phew." Charles rubbed his face and eyes hard with both hands. He leant back in the chair and closed his eyes.

Charles was in his office a few days later, looking at a plan on a drawing board. He wasn't particularly interested in a new bridge development. Well, not at that moment. Too many thoughts were drifting through his mind. A possible transfer. Dorothy's black water fever. Was the baby going to be all right? His gambling problems. "Blood, bloody hell," he said out loud to himself. He was jolted out of his misery by the phone ringing. It was Twiggy Branch.

"Yes, right. Thanks Twiggy. I'll be there right away." Charles placed the receiver gently on its cradle. Dorothy was in labour, three weeks early and they were moving her to a private ward in the maternity wing at the hospital. He sat in his chair for a moment. He didn't want to go to the hospital. There was nothing he could do right now anyway. He knew it. He was afraid.

It was nearly 4.30. Charles decided to call it a day. He drove back to the house and had his usual shower. He had to talk to someone. He explained Dorothy's situation to Jay and Girlie who listened intently and with great concern.

"I'll sleep at the hospital again tonight. Now, madam." Charles got down on his haunches and put Betty on his knee. "Your mother is having a baby so you will have a brother or sister to play with soon. Won't that be great?"

"I thought Mummy was sick? I want to see her Daddy." Betty sounded quiet and inquisitive.

"Well yes, she hasn't been well but she's also having a baby. Children are not allowed to visit in the hospital darling. Mummy will be home soon and we'll all be together. Now let Girlie bath you and I understand you'll be having your favourite scrambled egg and bacon for supper." Charles winked at Jay who beamed down at Betty. He hugged Betty and nudged her towards Girlie. Girlie was a big woman and picked her up with the greatest of ease and sat her on her forearm. "Come on little one, time for your bath."

Charles felt better having spoken to them and especially to Betty. He had been so wrapped up in his visits to the hospital, rushing back and forth between office, house and hospital, little Betty had taken back stage. He had also showered and changed into mufti. Yes, he felt much better.

Charles parked in the car park outside the hospital. He turned off the engine and looked at the hospital. It was only just dark and the lights outside the casualty department lit up the car park. He hated the place. He was reluctant to go in and had to force himself out of the car. He walked through the main doors. The kitchen must have been near the entrance as hideous combined smells of boiled cabbage and disinfectant greeted him. "Institutional cooking," he said to himself. He had no idea where the maternity wing was situated and stopped two nurses to enquire.

It sounded like a good five-minute walk. He was in no hurry. He was really hoping Dorothy would have had the baby by the time he got there. He was concerned about her condition and how she would handle the birth. Twiggy had been confident all would be all right.

He walked up the stairs to the second floor. He saw the notice board 'maternity department' and got a sinking feeling in his stomach. A tough looking woman came out of the office. She looked like a sergeant major, not only in stature and manner, but she had badges plastered all over her chest and epaulettes. She flew down the corridor, her white diamond-shaped headgear trailing behind in the updraft. "Hmmm," Charles said out loud to himself. "Hope she's not attending to Dorothy."

He nearly jumped out of his skin when he felt a hand on his shoulder. He turned around.

"Bloody hell Twiggy, you gave me the fright of my bloody life. How is Dorothy?"

"I've just this minute come out of the delivery room. She had your daughter half an hour ago. Don't worry Charles. She managed very well. She's a strong woman."

Charles put his hands to his face and muffled "Oh thank God for that. I've been beside myself."

"You're looking a bit pale around the gills yourself old boy. Come into the waiting room and I'll arrange for Sister to get you a cup of tea. When Dorothy's settled in her room you can see her, but only briefly Charles. She's very tired."

Twiggy had more news for Charles, not particularly good news. He had to tell him before he saw his new daughter. "Oh Sister, could you arrange for a cup of tea for the Major please? We'll be in the waiting room here." Twiggy lead him into the room.

"Dorothy has been extremely ill the last few months and as I've told you both, foetal retardation is not uncommon in cases of pregnant patients with ....."

"What's wrong with the baby? Blast it, what's wrong?" Charles was envisaging his new baby with two heads or three arms. Even no arms crossed his mind. "What is it?"

"Calm down Charles. It's something minor. Your daughter has no fingers on her right hand. She is perfectly formed in all other respects. A perfect young lass."

"I've got to see them." Charles left the waiting room and stood like a fool in the passage. He realised he didn't know where Dorothy's room was. Twiggy came to his rescue and they walked to the last room in the corridor.

"Just hang on a moment Charles," and Twiggy popped his head around the door. He looked back at Charles, smiled and gave the thumbs up.

Charles' heart was pounding, his mouth dry. Damn it he thought. He should have had a bunch of flowers in his hand. He cleared his throat nervously, and looked around the door. He was surprised.

Dorothy was looking good. Her hair was neatly brushed and her lips were as red as cherries. She was propped up in the bed and was holding a little bundle in her arms.

"Hello darling." Charles was nervous. Stupid, he thought. He walked over to her and kissed her on her forehead. He realised Twiggy and the two nurses had left the room. "How are you feeling?"

"Surprisingly well darling." Dorothy didn't want to waste any time. "Do you want to see our little Diana?" and at the same time pulled the shawl back and exposed a tiny little face.

"She's as beautiful as you my love and a true blonde too. I bet you she's got your blue eyes."

Dorothy wanted to tell him more. "Did they tell you about her little hand?" She wanted to show him and she gently removed Diana's right arm from the tightly wrapped shawl. "Isn't it so tiny and beautiful?" Dorothy was smiling at Charles and clearly wasn't concerned with her baby's missing fingers.

"Gosh, yes. Such a tiny hand! She has her thumb though, but so minute. There are little stubs where the fingers should have been."

"The staff said she had a 'deformity' but I don't want to think of it as that. It's just a special little part of our Diana. It's unique to her and special." Dorothy had totally accepted Diana's missing fingers. "Anyway, I think we're very blessed and lucky that it wasn't worse. I had been thinking of all sorts of horrid things the last few months."

Their little love bubble burst when the butch looking Sister with the air of a sergeant major stormed into the room, her head veil still bouncing wildly behind her. A nervous looking young nurse accompanied her.

"Good evening Major. Your wife has had a difficult few hours and we're taking the baby to the nursery so your wife can rest".

Charles wanted to stay with Dorothy as he had done in the other ward. He was sure the 'sergeant major' wouldn't allow it. She was talked about frequently in the Officers Mess and the chaps always said she was a force to be reckoned with. But he thought he would give it a try.

"Ah, Sister. I've been sleeping in the ward with my wife during her illness and I'd like to stay with her..." What he thought would happen, happened. Mrs Tough Cookie didn't hesitate to interrupt.

"Not a chance Major. I run an efficient ward and I'm not having it look like a boarding house. Your good wife will be fine and if there are any problems we will telephone you, which is normal hospital procedure."

Charles was highly annoyed to say the least. He knew he could override her decision but he realised Dorothy was a lot better, better than he thought she'd be and in any event, he wasn't prepared to argue with the old hag.

"I'm delighted you're so much better darling. And well done. Our Diana is beautiful. I'll see you tomorrow."

CHAPTER 3

Hong Kong 1928. Diana was six years old. Betty was eight. They now had a sister, Barbara, who was four. Barbara was born in Hong Kong, shortly after Charles' transfer there. Charles and Dorothy had fallen in love with Kandi and both had been reluctant to move to Hong Kong. Charles' batman, Jay, was able to transfer with Charles. Girlie was their private maid and the girls' nanny and she was happy to go with them to Hong Kong. She loved the girls and was almost part of the family.

Hong Kong had brought them a new life but also new problems. Horse racing was a major sport in the British Colony. But it wasn't just a sport for Charles. It became his life, so much so that his beloved family came second in his life. He wasn't able to control his speculative habit and he knew it and it was ruining him and his family. He spent so much time phoning the bookies that he frequently got behind with his work. He worked late to catch up then couldn't resist the back street gambling houses. Playing poker with the boys in the Sergeants Mess in India and Ceylon was child's play compared to the uncontrollable cancer that was now eating him alive. He would arrive home at 1 or 2am most mornings.

Dorothy gave up waiting for him to come home. They virtually lived separate lives. She continued to finance his cancerous addiction. She had no choice, short of leaving him or worse, divorcing him. He lavished Dorothy with an endless supply of gifts for her and their home. The children had the best clothing available. It was futile asking him to stop.

Charles would use his salary on family necessities and if there was any left over, it went on his nightly escapades. When he ran out of money, he borrowed and borrowed and still borrowed. It became a vicious, uncontrollable merry go round. A never-ending roller coaster.

Dorothy was accustomed to various individuals knocking on their door. It was invariably their last resort. They had reached the end of their patience trying to pin down Charles and thought their safest bet was to find him at home. Many a time he had these men in his study, tempers flared and doors slammed. Like a continual pumping oil well, Dorothy had to bail him out each time. Fortunately the inheritance from Dorothy's father was miraculously elasticised. She knew it wouldn't last forever but Charles was oblivious to it.

Despite their ups and downs Charles and Dorothy had a deep love for each other. Dorothy gave him his dues. He came home late but she knew, she just knew, sixth sense, honesty between them, call it what you will, there was no other woman in Charles' life.

She had made new friends, played tennis and kept a beautiful garden. She kept herself busy. Betty and Diana attended a private English school a few blocks from their house and Dorothy and Girlie took it in turns to do the school runs, which involved a ten minute walk through one of the most affluent leafy suburbs of Hong Kong. The house was perched high on a hill overlooking the harbour with beautiful views day and night.

Charles sat at his office desk. Work was piling up. There were three major surveys in his pending tray, which should have been completed by now. The phone rang. He assumed who it might be and he was right. Someone after their money. He made his usual promises, which were invariably as empty as a colander under a running tap.

"Damn creditors," Charles said to himself. "They should be called predators, more to the bloody point."

He leant back in his chair, his hands behind his head. He knew his life was in a mess. Bookies, horse racing, roulette, all controlling his life. He couldn't damn well stop. It wasn't a game between him and Dorothy either. Charles didn't comprehend the gravity of the situation and was nonchalant, almost oblivious to it at times. It was just Charles, just his way of life. It was Dorothy's elasticised inheritance that kept his creditors at bay and that too had become routine. Being an engineer he should have been aware that elastic, when pulled continuously to capacity, will eventually break. It has to. It's the law of averages.

Charles was brought back to reality when the phone rang. Bookie or predator he thought. He picked it up. "Hello? Ahum. Good afternoon Brigadier." Why the hell, Charles thought to himself, was 'egg on legs' phoning him? The Brigadier never phoned him. They invariably corresponded by letter. "Yes Sir. Certainly. 8.30 tomorrow morning." He put the phone back on its cradle very slowly, deep in thought.

'Egg on legs' was the Commanding Officer for the entire region. He was bestowed with the nickname because of his all too weird shape with his huge waist and skinny short legs, which dangled precariously from his necessarily outsized uniform shorts. He was so wide the local community believed a whole cow was used to make up his leather belt and Sam brown.

Charles pushed himself to take a folder out of his pending tray and he opened a large plan. He couldn't concentrate. It was nearly 4.30 and he wanted to be with Dorothy. All of sudden he didn't want to head downtown for his nightly ritual.

He decided to drive home via the back roads and wanted to avoid the hustle and bustle of down town Hong Kong. He wasn't in the mood to drive cautiously through narrow streets, unruly pedestrians, rickshaws and endless rows of shop stalls. He took the scenic route through affluent suburbia, huge colonial style houses sparsely placed on either side of the roads. Neatly clipped lawns swept down on both sides of the road with colourful hydrangeas and geraniums thoughtfully placed and it looked like a highway to heaven.

Needless to say Dorothy was cautiously surprised to see Charles home at a civilised hour. "Charles you must be sick! What a nice surprise." She didn't intend to be sarcastic. It wasn't in her make up.

They both enjoyed a quiet evening and a game of chess. "Let's sit on the veranda for a while." Dorothy did so on her own most evenings and often wished Charles was with her to enjoy the view. She got up from the chess table and held out her hand to him. "Come," she said quietly.

It was serene and cosy up on the hill. The only sound was the wind rushing through the palm trees in the garden. It was secluded and private with the nearest homestead two hundred yards away. They had uninterrupted views of the harbour, the shoreline demarcated at night by the lights on the junks hugging the shore. Lights flickering from anchored cargo boats near the horizon added to the lustrous vista.

"I could stay here forever." Dorothy leant against Charles on their swing seat.

Charles didn't answer. He was still wondering why the Brigadier wanted to see him. He wasn't in the mood to tell Dorothy. He would, but not now. He never kept anything from her now, even his gambling. She knew all about that.

The sky above them and the garden lit up briefly. A few seconds later thunder rumbled behind the house.

"There's a storm brewing. Shall we hit the hay and listen to the rain on the roof?" Charles put his arm around Dorothy's shoulders and kissed her on her cheek.

Charles was in bed before Dorothy. He watched her sitting at her dressing table. First a cream, then it was wiped off. Then something else and that was wiped off too. Then yet another cream. Then a hairnet to keep the curls in place.

"A thing of beauty is a joy forever," joked Charles.

Dorothy jumped into bed next to him like a five year old. "You never see all this because you're forever dealing out cards or watching those silly balls going aimlessly round and round those roulette wheels or whatever you call them." Dorothy giggled and kissed him briefly.

He grabbed her around the waist and pushed her onto her back. Their sex, when they had it, was still as good as on their wedding night, if not better. They both believed that was the best recipe for a good marriage, coupled with total honesty, in and out of bed. If there wasn't that, something would snap eventually.

The rain pelted down on the tin roof. It was almost deafening. They loved the sound. They lay in each other's arms in the dark, lightning flashes illuminating the room occasionally.

Charles woke early. He immediately had a sinking feeling in his stomach and he knew the impending meeting with the Brigadier woke him, not so much his unusually early night. He brushed his teeth and went into the kitchen to make himself a cup of coffee. He went out onto the veranda and sat on the edge of the swing. The sun was just breaking the horizon, half a red ball sitting on the sea. He sipped his coffee and thought about egg on legs. "What does the fart want?" Charles was at ease talking to himself.

"Who's the fart?" Dorothy stood in her dressing gown with her hands clasped around a cup of coffee and sounded vaguely intrigued in a sleepy way. She sat beside him, also on the edge of the swing, mimicking him.

"Old egg on legs phoned me yesterday and wants to see me at 8.30."

Dorothy knew who he was talking about. "Did he say why?"

"No. No indication. I don't know what the hell it's about." Charles sounded a little anxious.

Deep down they both had a pretty good idea why the Brigadier wanted to see him but neither of them wanted to think about it, let alone talk about it.

The sun had pierced the horizon completely now and globules of water shone on the ruby red bougainvillea flowers, like little eyes looking out to sea. The sun rose by the minute and as it did so the eyes could see further out to sea, calm and glassy after the storm the night before.

"Bye darling. Let me know what his Lordship has to say," Dorothy kissed him through the car window.

Charles drove to the army camp where his office was located. The army headquarters for the Far East was also located in the camp barely a five minute drive from Charles' office. Needless to say the Brigadier was based at army HQ.

Charles went to his office first, to get his mind into gear. He wasn't sure what gear it was in but he wanted to steady his nerves. 8.15. He had better leave.

He stood outside the Brigadiers office. It was 8.25. Charles felt like a schoolboy outside the headmaster's office, waiting for a caning. The old Brigadier was a formidable chap actually. He didn't take crap from anyone and always went by the book. One couldn't fault him. Well, except his shape. Charles grinned to himself.

A Lieutenant came out of a door marked Chief Clerk, right next to the Brigadier's office, bang on 8.30. "Good morning Major. The Brigadier will see you now." He opened the door for Charles. Charles marched in, stood to attention and saluted the very round fat man sitting at a large desk.

"Sir," snapped Charles.

"Sit down Major. This won't take long."

Charles removed his cap and chose to sit in a hard upright chair.

"I'll get to the point Major. This office has received three letters of complaint, final demands actually, in the last week from reputable members of the community. You owe these men an awful lot of money, in fact more than you and I would even earn in an entire year. I had a call from London last week as well. Someone in Hong Kong wrote anonymously to the Minister of Defence complaining about your gambling debts. Whilst we object to anonymous letters, clearly people are agitated and concerned about monies owing to them. We have been aware of your gambling habits. However, we were not aware of the magnitude of your debt. This cannot be tolerated within the army, especially commissioned ranks. What have you to say for yourself Major?"

What could he say? He felt like a caged animal. Snared. Caught. He thought he had been playing his cards close to his chest and wasn't aware old egg on legs had his finger on the pulse. Charles was more than annoyed his creditors had written to HQ.

"I always settle my debts, Sir, and these will be settled as well."

"And how do you propose paying these vast amounts?" The Brigadier was going red in the face.

"Um, my wife has a little money in England and we can arrange payment in a week or so."

"This problem of your stems back a good ten years, to India and Ceylon. You have had previous warnings, duly recorded in your record of service. You're an embarrassment to the army let alone the bloody Empire! You are to be discharged from His Majesty's Services. This directive has come from the Ministry of Defence in London. Your three months notice will commence today. That's all Major."

"Sir, if I settle…   ." Charles was plunged into silence.

"You are to be discharged from the army. The chief clerk has the details. That is all, Major."

No point fighting city hall Charles thought to himself. He put on his cap, stood to attention and gave a swift salute.

"Sir" snapped Charles again, did a sharp about turn and marched from the room. He gave the chief clerk's office a wide birth and headed for his car. "Damn it, damn it, damn it," Charles muttered to himself.

Charles went home at 4.30. It was the second night he wasn't interested in going downtown. Whether he went or not, it was too late. The damage was done. He sat in the car outside the house. Who was that bastard who wrote anonymously to London he thought. He sighed. How was he going to tell Dorothy? She loved Hong Kong. So did he. What about the girls? What the hell were they to do? His mind was racing.

He went into the house. He heard chatter and laughter in the kitchen. He stood at the kitchen door and saw his beautiful daughters. All three had their hands in a huge mixing bowl on the table; they were up to their elbows in flour and brown cake mix. Barbara was too small to reach the bowl and was standing on a wooden stool whilst Girlie steadied her. Dorothy was greasing a cake tin.

"My my my. What do we have here? Cordon bleu chefs in the making eh?" Charles smiled at Dorothy.

Dorothy was quick to explain the chaos. "We're making a

chocolate cake for Diana's seventh birthday tomorrow. Seven. Can you believe it! How are you darling?"

"I'm parched. I'd love a cup of tea. Can I have a word with you darling?" Charles suddenly felt an urgent need to tell Dorothy what had happened. She was a level headed woman and he drew strength from her.

Dorothy sensed something was wrong. "Girlie, can you carry on and help the girls get the cake into the oven please?"

"Yes Mrs Butler. I'll bring you a tray of tea." Girlie had been their maid for nearly ten years and she too knew something wasn't right.

Dorothy and Charles sat on the veranda where they found sanctuary and peace. It was a muggy afternoon after the storm last evening. The sun had done a one hundred and eighty degree turn since they had sat there in the morning. A huge red ball hung precariously above the horizon falling almost noticeably to its inevitable resting place in the bowels of the ocean. The sky was bright crimson with hints of purple and red with dozens of strips of pink cloud lying horizontally and motionless across the sky and that red ball.

"A red sky at night," were Charles' first words after minutes of silence.

"Is a shepherd's delight," finished Dorothy. Girlie had brought their tray of tea. "Thank you Girlie. A plate of sandwiches too. You're spoiling us. Will you bath the girls and get supper ready?"

"And no chocolate cake until they're finished their supper. We decided to make two, one for pudding tonight and one for the party tomorrow," chuckled Girlie. She had her usual friendly spunk about her.

"What is it Charles? What's wrong? You're home early two

nights in a row, which tells me something. I know you too well. What's happened?" Dorothy sounded stern.

"Oh Christ Dorothy. I'm in the crap. Right in it, up to my bloody neck." Charles knew he could talk openly to Dorothy. He relied on her and trusted her explicitly. He was never shy or embarrassed talking to her. "I saw Mr bloody 'egg on legs' this morning. In a nutshell, I've been fired. Kicked out of the army. Three months notice from today. Unemployed and no fixed abode on the 12th August."

Dorothy didn't answer. She didn't really have to. It had happened at last. His gambling had got the better of him and she knew it would happen eventually. They both sat silently for a few minutes. The sun had changed colour and its purple head was slipping behind the earth's bulge, barely visible now in the late spring haze.

"Needless to say Charles, all to do with your gambling." Dorothy made a statement and wasn't questioning him.

"HQ has received three final demands and he tells me some bastard wrote to London – to the Minister of Defence no less, belly aching about my debts. The letter was anonymous apparently. It could have been anyone but I wish I knew who the hell it was. I'd wring his bloody neck." Charles gazed blankly out to sea.

"You've really put your foot in it this time. I suppose I can blame myself in some respects for having fuelled your blasted addiction. What would you have done, had I not kept bailing you out?" Dorothy sounded deflated.

"Probably been behind bars a long time ago." He was fed up and feeling irritable.

Dorothy was feeling far from comfortable. "I suppose I'll have to contact my bank in London and do the necessary *again*. Operation normal. Really Charles, I'm getting just a little fed up with all this. It just goes on and on. It never damn well stops. What's the damage this time?" She seldom lost her rag but she was almost at her wits end with him.

"I don't know. I think it's in the region of £6,000." There was a sense of remorse in his voice.

"What?" Dorothy shouted. Her outburst was involuntary. "You're joking. You must be bloody joking."

"I wish I bloody well was," replied Charles quietly.

"That's it. I've had enough Charles. Enough is enough. You can go to bloody hell." Dorothy stormed into the house like a raging tornado.

The following weeks were rough for both of them. They barely spoke to each other. Charles surprisingly, was home by 5 o'clock every day. He spent his evenings in his study whilst Dorothy played patience in the sitting room. It was their nightly ritual. The children were oblivious to their problems and Dorothy had no intention of mentioning them to her girls. They were far too young.

Dorothy never concentrated on her games of patience. She was quite content to be on her own in the evenings as it gave her time and space to think. She had not spoken to Charles about his mounting debt. Clearly it worried her and she knew in her heart of hearts she would have to settle them. She was intentionally putting off the evil moment. She wanted him to think about it and sweat, which seemed to be working, because she had never seen Charles so quiet and withdrawn. Had he learnt his lesson this time? Never she thought.

He had cost her a small fortune over the years. She knew her father's inheritance was dwindling rapidly and there would be very little left after forking out the £6,000 owing on his latest gambling frenzy. The supposedly bottomless pit was almost empty and Dorothy's stomach turned. What the hell will they do when it *does* run out? She perished the thought and didn't want to think about it but she had to be realistic. They had three girls to bring up and educate and above all she wanted them to enjoy the lifestyle they were accustomed to. She was deep in her thoughts when Charles' voice brought her back to earth with an unpleasant bump. She was enjoying her space and her ability to think her life through.

"Tea, darling?" Charles' voice was almost a whisper. He had a small tray, set with one teacup.

She really wasn't in the mood to talk to him. She was wrapped up in her thoughts and she didn't want to get involved in small talk with him. "Just leave it there." She was abrupt and pointed to a small table next to her.

Charles got the message loud and clear. She certainly wasn't ready to talk to him. "I think I'll be off to bed."

Dorothy didn't answer him. She was devastated. He had ruined his career in the army and he was ruining his family.

Another two gruelling weeks passed and the household was taking on the characteristics of a mortuary. Even Betty and Diana had asked Dorothy what was wrong with their Mummy and Daddy. Girlie and Jay had noticed too but they knew it was not for them to make any comments or ask questions. Dorothy had always been open with Girlie and Girlie wondered why she was not offering an explanation.

Dorothy knew she had to break the ice eventually. Charles wasn't in a position to do it. He knew Dorothy wouldn't budge until she was ready and he had to rely on her to offer the olive branch, if she was willing to do that. Over the past month, Charles had been harassed by his creditors. They had phoned him almost on a daily basis at the office and they were threatening to take legal action. Charles kept stalling by assuring them the money was coming from London. He had no idea if Dorothy had arranged funds from her London account. He knew he had cooked his goose with her and couldn't bring himself to ask her. That would have been the final straw. He had to wait it out.

It was now six weeks before Charles would be out of the army. Time had flown and they had achieved nothing in trying to decide what to do with their lives after that. Their nightly routine was becoming a habit and still little conversation took place between them. Dorothy realised it couldn't go on and she was conditioning herself into talking to Charles again.

As usual, she was in the sitting room after supper with her pack of cards for company. She heard a car drive up to the front of the house and a car door slammed. She heard footsteps come up the wooden steps and onto the veranda. They stopped. She heard a strong knock on the front door. Who the hell is that, she thought.

She knew Charles was in the study next to the sitting room and had obviously heard their unknown visitor arriving as well. She was right as she heard Charles open the study door, walk along the passage and into the hallway. Dorothy heard muffled voices but couldn't hear what was being said. The voices continued for a few minutes then she heard the front door closing. Charles walked back to his study and she heard the door close.

Dorothy played another game of patience. She was itching to know who their visitor was but she couldn't bring herself to talk to Charles. She could be as stubborn as a mule if she wanted to be.

She heard the study door open. Good, she thought, he's made the first move. The sitting room door didn't open. "Damn it. Probably went to the bathroom," Dorothy whispered to herself.

Ten minutes later the sitting room door opened and Charles came in with another peace offering, hoping it would work this time.

"Thank you." Dorothy sounded more amenable than usual and Charles breathed a sigh of relief. "Two cups tonight I see."

Charles gave a nervous short laugh. "Well, yes," he hesitated. "Ever hopeful." He didn't know what else to say and didn't want to fluff his inroads. "Can I be mother?"

"Yes please. Not too much milk for me." Dorothy was finding it a bit easier but she also wanted to know who had been at the door. She couldn't contain her curiosity and she knew Charles would be receptive. "Who was at the door?"

Charles wanted to tell her but he was afraid how she would react. He hesitated for a moment, cautious how to word it. His sense of honesty and forthrightness came to the fore, as was his usual wont with her. "It was the clerk of the civil court." He stopped momentarily. "He served a summons for me to appear in court next week. It's a civil writ. Those three chaps have gone the whole hog, obviously went to their lawyers and are demanding their £6,000." He had mixed feelings. He was glad he had got it off his chest but was terrified how his beloved would react. He loved her and didn't want to lose her.

Dorothy sat silently, both hands clasped around her teacup as she stared uninterested at her hand of cards on the table. She was quiet for a few minutes and Charles was beginning to feel uneasy. He sipped his tea nervously.

Dorothy took a deep breath. She remained quiet for a few moments. "I don't know Charles. What are we going to do?" She knew it was a pointless question. She knew exactly what would happen. "I suppose I will have to foot the bloody bill again." She could feel her blood pressure going through the roof. She knew she had to calm down. Another confrontation wasn't going to solve the problem. "Charles, I am running out of money. I don't know if that makes sense to you. I don't have much left. I'm trying to tell you in plain, simple English. If I pay this I will have very little left and I won't be able to get you out of the muck again." Dorothy remained calm and to the point. She had more to say. "If it ever happens again, I will leave you Charles and I'll go back to England with the girls. I mean it Charles. I won't have you wreck their lives."

Charles felt no relief with her offer. He was devastated that he was hurting the only person he had loved with such passion. They were both silent for a long time.

Dorothy broke the silence again. "I'll wire the bank in the morning. The transfer will take a few days. It should be here before the bloody court date."

Charles took a long time to respond. "Dorothy. You have no idea what you and the girls mean to me. You are my life, my reason for breathing. I'm just heartbroken that I've hurt you. I think you know that. My problem has been an illness I suppose. It's been something I haven't been able to control. This latest incident has scared me. I was afraid of losing you and that's the last thing I want. I promise you I'll do everything in my power to stop."

Dorothy had to drum home her circumstances, which were in her interests as well as his. "I can't reiterate or emphasise this enough. I am running out of money." She said the last sentence slowly and decisively. "I'm going to say it again Charles. I am running out of money. I won't be able to do this again, even if I want to. We will be out on the streets, begging."

Dorothy's bank obliged as they normally did and Charles was able to present a cheque to the clerk of the civil court the day before the court hearing. The case was duly erased from the civil roll and the court file closed.

Another chapter closed in Charles' life thought Dorothy, but she lived in perpetual fear of what he would do next and where it would take their lives.

Girlie put the mail on the kitchen table having collected it from their letterbox at the end of the driveway. Dorothy was in the kitchen concocting a concentrated cool drink for the girls. They loved lemon juice and sugar and iced water when they got home from school.

She noticed a foreign stamp on one of the envelopes and took a closer look. It was from Africa and addressed to Charles. Dorothy was intrigued but wasn't going to open mail addressed to him. She'd have to contain herself until he got home.

True to his word, Charles was home each evening at 5 o'clock and tonight was no exception.

Dorothy greeted him in the passage and wasted no time. She had the letter in her hand. "I'm fascinated by this letter from Africa. Please open it!" She was like a child on Christmas Day.

Charles went into their bedroom and took off his stuffy tunic and put on a cotton shirt and shorts. He joined Dorothy in their favourite spot. "I recognise the writing. I think it's from Sir Edmund." Charles used the end of a teaspoon and opened the letter carefully and lent back on the swing. It was only two pages and didn't take him long. "Hmm. Interesting. Very interesting." There was an air of excitement in his voice.

"What is it? What does he say?" Dorothy sat on a folded leg and jumped up and down on the swing. "Can I read it?"

"Hang on, hang on." Charles sounded happy and held the letter above him out of Dorothy's reach. "You know that Sir Edmund was transferred to Africa from India. Well I wrote to him a few months ago when all this nonsense flared up and asked him if he could put out a few feelers for me on the job front. He gave my credentials to an engineering company and they want me!"

"Let me see, let me see," Dorothy grabbed the letter from Charles. "Oh, he says the company will write to you! Sounds exciting. Africa! Heavens, what do you think Charles?"

"It will be great. We'll start a new life. There'll be no chance of gambling there! Apparently there are lots of new opportunities and development going on."

Dorothy came down to earth. "I wonder what the schooling will be like for the girls. Oh gosh, we were going to stay in Hong Kong and we were going to rent a house for now."

"Darling, someone here was after my guts. Some bastard stuck a knife in my back when he wrote to London. You know that. As much as we love it, I don't particularly want to go into civilian life here knowing there's a snake out there who might strike again and it could be for another reason. I just don't like the prospect. There are some good schools in Africa, a lot run by missionaries."

"It does sound exciting, doesn't it? Shall we pop a cork tonight?"

Charles was over the moon with Dorothy's excitement.

The house looked like a warehouse. Boxes were piled high, furniture wrapped with cardboard and bound with rope and an air of excitement and expectation abounded. Dorothy, Jay and Girlie hadn't stopped in weeks and Charles did his bit in the evenings as well. The girls never stopped asking questions. They knew they were going to Africa and wanted to know every detail. What would it be like, what would the school be like, what would their new house look like. Their inquisitiveness was endless and invariably Dorothy couldn't give them a decisive answer, not because she didn't want to, but she was as much in the dark as they were. But they all knew it would be a new life and an adventure into the unknown.

Charles had received a letter from his new employer days after receiving the good news from Sir Edmund. The company, based in Nairobi, Kenya had offered to pay for Charles' relocation, including the shipping of their furniture and the fares for the entire family on a ship bound for England. They were to disembark at Mombassa on the East coast of Africa. Charles had successfully negotiated the inclusion of Girlie in the company's package. They had asked her to join them and she agreed, much to the delight of everyone and especially the girls. Girlie was part of the family and they all perished the thought of parting. Jay was to remain at the house and was to be batman to the army officer replacing Charles. Jay had been with him from India days and there was an air of sadness around. He had elected to take the day off on the day they left and said he would head for downtown Hong Kong to try and take his mind off their departure.

It was the 12th August, the day Charles and Dorothy dreaded and a day they thought would never happen. Charles was being discharged from the army. The ship taking them to their new life was leaving Hong Kong on the 16th August and the army had allowed them to remain in their government house until they left. Charles didn't have a penny to his name but of course they were accustomed to that. Their relocation was funded totally by his new employer. Charles had arranged for the finance clerk at HQ to forward his final salary cheque to his new company. Every little helped.

Charles and Dorothy were cautiously excited on the day of their departure. Their last night in the house had been quiet – and empty. They rattled around and their footsteps echoed throughout the house, their furniture already despatched to the ship. The army quartermaster had loaned them camp beds and bedding for their last few nights. They cooked on a small paraffin stove also On His Majesty's Service.

Betty, Diana and Barbara were immaculately dressed as was Girlie. They were waiting on the veranda for over two hours before their taxi was due. There was lots of chatter and laughter and they seemed unconcerned at leaving the house that had been home to them for so long, the thoughts of the ship and a new continent were far more important now.

Dorothy and Charles did a systematic check through each room in the house to ensure everything was clean and that they had left nothing behind. They went outside to join the children and Girlie. Their timing was spot on as the taxi arrived minutes later. Their furniture was to accompany them on the ship and they hoped they would travel with it overland to Nairobi. But that was weeks away and they wanted to spend time together on the ship, relax and take in the sun.

The ship dwarfed them as they made their way along the quay, the smell of the sea, fish and oil culminating into customary dockside smells. It was a British mail ship and made regular journeys between the Far East and England carrying passengers and cargo. Charles saw a large notice on a building near the ship, marked Customs and Immigration.

"Come on darling. Let's clear customs and immigration." Charles showed his family into the building, and with all the paper work in order, led his team to the side of the ship and elected to go up first. Charles had a suitcase in each hand and walked up the gangplank, which swayed slightly as the family followed eagerly behind. Girlie took up the rear and she too was weighed down with a suitcase in each hand.

A member of the crew showed them to their cabins. They had been allocated three cabins, all next door to each other as they had requested. A major debate had already taken place some weeks ago between the girls and Girlie and there had been a consensus on the sleeping arrangements. Betty and Diana would be together and Barbara would share with Girlie.

"I'm delighted we've got outside cabins," said Dorothy as she peeped out of the porthole.

"Yes. I was quite sure we'd be given an inner cabin. The new boss is obviously a generous old fellow. Anyway, one gets quite claustrophobic in those inner cabins. Shall we go on deck?"

"Let's check on the girls." Dorothy went into the cabin next to theirs and Betty and Diana had their heads at the porthole both trying to look out at the same time. The cabin looked cosy and more than adequate for the girls. Charles checked the porthole was permanently sealed. Good, he thought to himself. There was an inter-leading door between the girls' cabins, which was ideal. It was probably designed as a family suite and of course Girlie would be able to keep an eye on them.

"That's an ideal set up. Are you happy with your cabin Barbara, Girlie? They're rather fun and cosy aren't they?" Dorothy was very happy the girls were nearby.

"Come on everyone. We're going on deck. I feel as though I'm in a harem with all these women around me." Charles smacked Dorothy on her rump.

The girls ran along the corridor like a herd of wild animals and Girlie had to rein them in. They stood on the deck and watched the quayside workers doing last minute chores. Everyone must have been on board as a crane lifted the gangplank away from the side of the ship. The quayside was full of family and friends saying their goodbyes to the passengers.

"There's the Blue Peter." Charles looked up on one of the masts near a funnel stack where the flag had been hoisted.

"What's the Blue Peter?" asked Diana.

"It's the name of the flag a ship flies shortly before setting sail," said Charles.

The ropes were released from the quay and two tugs stood by, one either end of the ship, ready to guide her out of her bay. There was a long hoot and the ship shuddered, a strong solid shudder as the starboard propeller was thrown into action.

The gap between the quayside and the side of the ship widened and the railings started to vibrate. A small stream of black smoke now rose from the chimneystack as the tug near the bows started to position herself and nudge the huge ship further away from the quay, until she was facing the vast ocean. The port propeller was activated, joining its partner and the water swirled like a boiling witches cauldron and the shuddering intensified as smoke thickened from the funnel stack.

Diana clung to her mother's hand and Dorothy felt her little hand in hers. She grasped it with both hands and gave it a loving rub. She loved Diana and her little deformed hand. They were all so accustomed to it now no one noticed it. Dorothy felt tears welling in her eyes and she was grateful for Diana and her safe birth despite her own grave illness those seven long years ago.

The bows sliced effortlessly through the turquoise water, which looked greener on some days than others. Then there would be patches of deep blue then green as though an undecided artist had swept his brush across a canvas. The ship rolled gently as she steamed westwards towards Africa, the throb of the engines monotonous yet giving a sense of adventure and purpose.

On the second last day of their trip, Dorothy and Charles were woken as usual by the cabin porter with their morning tray of tea. There was something different that morning. The porter was anxious and spoke decisively and quickly.

"Captain tells us we're heading into a tropical storm. The sea's pretty rough out there this morning." The porter was holding the tray with great concentration as he tried to steady himself in the doorway of their cabin. "You had better keep a hold of the tray sir or it will end up on the floor." He put the tray on a chest of drawers next to Charles' bed and couldn't let go until Charles held the tray. From their bed they could see the ship was rolling; one minute they saw the sea from their porthole and the next minute blue sky.

Dorothy decided the girls should get dressed and get on deck. Dorothy and Charles had travelled on ships before, albeit on their own and before they had met, aware that the best thing to do when the sea is rough is to get on deck to avoid bouts of seasickness.

Dorothy dressed and went into Betty and Diana's cabin to find Girlie had taken the bull by the horns and had told the girls to dress. All four were in the one cabin, Betty looking decidedly pale and they looked nervously at Dorothy.

"The sea looks rough today Mrs Butler. What do you want us to do?" Girlie was looking for support.

"This is exciting Mummy. Can we go up and look at the sea?" Diana was sitting on the bunk, which was probably the safest place to be. The others were holding on to bits of fixed furniture as the ship rolled from side to side.

"It will be better if we all go on deck. We'll feel better up there."

Dorothy led the gang out of the cabin and along the corridor. They were flung in unison from one side of the corridor to the other and stopped on occasions, feet strategically apart to steady themselves. They felt more comfortable as they climbed the steps at the end of the corridor, able to cling to the rails. Then up another set of steps, then another until they could smell the sea air.

There was very little blue sky now and thick black clouds had gathered around them, with huge cumulus clouds towering tens of thousands of feet above the sea. The weather had certainly changed and the wind was reacting to the brewing storm as it churned the sea, like an orchestra responding to its conductor. It had started raining ahead of the ship and the blanket of rain hung like a massive grey blind pulled down from the black turbulent clouds swirling above. It looked threatening and ominous and as the ship rolled and pitched, sailors ran around the deck collecting chairs that had been flung in all directions.

It was too rough to remain on deck and passengers had gathered in the lounges on deck, protected from the weather by thick glass. Dorothy and Charles headed for one of the lounges, the children and Girlie herded together. A senior officer clad in a white uniform with volumes of gold braid on his epaulette was addressing the passengers.

"The Captain is not concerned about the storm. We have encountered much worse but it is obviously of concern to you and we would like to alleviate any of your worries. The storm is at its peak now and we do not anticipate it getting any worse. Breakfast is now being served and those with strong stomachs are requested to make their way to the dining room."

The passengers appreciated his joke and there was spontaneous laughter and clapping. About twenty passengers took up his offer including Charles' brood, Dorothy and Girlie. They all had a strong constitution and they weren't going to allow the storm get the better of them.

They dillydallied over breakfast as there wasn't much else to do with the decks out of bounds during the storm. An hour and a half was spent in the dining room and they noticed the rolling and pitching of the ship had subsided. With stomachs full of cereal, fruit, eggs, bacon and toast and copious cups of coffee, they ventured up on deck again.

A pleasant transformation confronted them. The grey mass of rain and towering cumulus clouds were on the horizon behind the ship and numerous wisps of cirrus hung high in the sky above them. A few miles ahead, almost as though a rubber had been swept across the sky, the line of cirrus stopped and blue sky beckoned. They stood on the deck and watched the sea. The colour varied from dark blue behind them where the storm was petering out to tropical blue beyond the bows where the suns rays had found their way beyond the cirrus cloud. Dorothy wondered if it was a good omen and would it mean a bright new life in Africa. She was brought back to earth when Charles slipped his arm around her waist.

"Penny for your thoughts," Charles whispered in her ear.

"Oh, they're priceless. Not for sale. We arrive in Africa tomorrow. The time has flown by. I hope someone's there to meet us."

"Everything was confirmed, and they're aware of our arrival date. Everything will fall into place," Charles reassured her.

CHAPTER 4

Nairobi, Kenya. 1928. They had been in Kenya for nearly four months. It was magical, absolute bliss, heaven on earth. Charles had turned over a new leaf and had remained true to his word and avoided the pestilent habit that had dominated their lives. Dorothy was elated and thought it was nothing short of miraculous. He had an extremely good salary, much more than he had earned in the army and his new boss John Harvey, director of the engineering company, did everything possible to ensure their comfort. Dorothy got back to her tennis and was heavily involved with charity work with Lady Mary. Sir Edmund was transferred to Kenya a few years earlier from India. He was again appointed Commanding Officer for the region and he and Lady Mary were well settled.

Charles had a company house in an affluent suburb on the outskirts of Nairobi. As with all their previous houses it was a rambling residence with the standard tropical veranda to cool and protect the house from the savage African sun. The house was enhanced by a manageable sized garden caringly maintained by the gardener, Sixpence and Dorothy. Sixpence and the three girls put the wooden crates from their journey to good use and constructed a superb tree house high in an acacia tree in the back garden, with windows tastefully curtained by Girlie from old dresses. Old corrugated iron sheets made a perfect roof and Charles erected a rope ladder enabling the girls to clamber up and down the tree like a troop of monkeys.

The company had a huge amount of work on its books. Kenya was a new British Colony and new ventures and businesses were springing up in the country. Houses, factories, buildings, bridges and railways were mushrooming everywhere and Dorothy and Charles were sure their future was secured for many years ahead.

Christmas Day was weeks away. The girls, Girlie and Dorothy decorated the tree in the sitting room after Dorothy and Sixpence had scoured the area and had found a healthy branch which they hack-sawed off the main trunk of a fir tree. They found an old paint tin in the garage, a left over from the previous tenants, filled it with sand and rocks and the tree stood very elegantly next to the fireplace. The girls took it in turns placing colourful balls on the tree. They had wrapped old matchboxes with colourful paper and tied them like parcels leaving a loop, enabling them to hang on the branches. Despite the intricate way the boxes were tied and looped, Diana managed to do her bit with her one and a half hands. It never ceased to amaze Girlie how she managed to tie the tiniest of bows and reef knots using her thumb and the little soft bump in place of her forefinger. They placed strips of white cotton material on top of the branches, and with a stretch of the imagination resembled a dusting of snow.

"Necessity is the mother of invention. That looks beautiful. First class. Well done everyone." Charles stood in the sitting room doorway admiring the tree.

"It looks good, doesn't it?" Dorothy stood back to admire their handy work. "Now, we've been mixing the Christmas cake. We waited for you to come home so we can all have a wish before putting it in the oven." Dorothy took him by the hand and they went into the kitchen followed by the troop, trailing behind like a row of monkeys. She removed the damp cloth from the bowl of cake mix and they took it in turns to stir the mixture with a big wooden spoon, each making a secret wish as they did so.

"That will take a good four hours to cook. Now everyone...." Dorothy was stopped by the girls.

"Don't slam the doors or the cake will sink," said Diana and Barbara in unison as though mimicking Dorothy. They all knew the routine.

Christmas Day was very much a family day, but they invited their old friends Sir Edmund and Lady Mary, as their children were now grown up and living in England. Dorothy and Girlie did most of the cooking with help from Diana, who was the most domesticated of the girls and loved cooking.

Charles was very busy at work. He impressed everyone he came into contact with, including other engineering companies and local government authorities. He was able to maintain fairly regular office hours and he and Dorothy enjoyed an excellent relationship.

Dorothy on the other hand enjoyed working with Girlie in the house and spent a lot of time designing various parts of the garden with new shrubs, flowerbeds and rock gardens. She worked well with Sixpence who also contributed to new ideas. She played tennis once a week and gave her time in the local community. The children attended a missionary school nearby and life was good, very good. Dorothy would never have dreamt that their lives could have changed for the better.

Charles was to attend a meeting in John Harvey's office. He knew nothing about it but knew some high-powered businessmen were attending. Charles arrived at Harvey's office fifteen minutes before the appointed time, at Harvey's request. Charles knocked on the door.

"Come in," was the muffled response.

Charles opened the door and went in. "Hello Mr Harvey."

"I would like to fill you in before the clients arrive, Charles. These chaps represent a consortium and they've asked us to prepare a plan for local government. They're keen to have a racecourse built in Nairobi. I'd like you to give them your views."

"Yes certainly." Charles was oblivious to the ramifications of such a project and merely thought of it as a challenge.

Four men attended the meeting with Harvey and Charles. They had produced a rough plan of their proposals, desired location, buildings required and length and shape of the course. It was agreed Charles would approach the local planning office prior to a full survey, to establish their willingness for such a project.

Charles wasted no time in seeing the local planning officer. The proposed site was available for use and was suitably positioned in relation to other projects already submitted to the planning office.

"We've been given the green light," Charles informed Harvey a few weeks later.

"Excellent. Can you get the land and course surveyed and in the meantime I'll inform our clients and they can give us a comprehensive idea of the buildings and stables they require. Let's go for it. This is going to be a great recreational sport for the local community."

The months passed. Everything was running smoothly in Charles' household but not in Charles and Dorothy's secret thoughts. Dorothy was well aware of the new racecourse being built and both of them never broached the subject, purposely. Deep down Dorothy was terrified of what might happen and Charles tried to put his worrying thoughts at the back of his mind. He knew it would never happen again. It just couldn't.

Charles had to tell Dorothy about the official opening. "We've been invited to the official opening of the race course next week. It's going to be quite an event apparently and the Governor will be attending."

"I don't care if the King himself attends," Dorothy sounded purposely disinterested.

"What do you mean?" asked Charles.

"It means I'm not going."

"You can't not go, darling. We've both been invited and it'll look pretty stupid if I go on my own." Charles was concerned.

"Tell them I'm sick," replied Dorothy.

"Be realistic. You are really taking this too far. It will be quite alright." Charles wanted to convince her.

"I told you Charles, I am *not* going. Subject closed." She was adamant.

Charles knew better than to get into an argument with his beloved. "You are worrying unnecessarily but if you don't want to go I can't force you but I will have to go. Harvey will expect me to be there."

Charles did go on his own. Dorothy didn't want to be part of his old habit, as though she condoned it.

The weeks ahead were gruelling for Dorothy. The horseracing had started and she heard from Sixpence and Girlie that it was drawing big crowds. She was always quietly delighted when she heard Charles' car in the driveway every afternoon. He was never late.

For several months he arrived home after work and he helped the children with their homework. Dorothy and Charles kept much to themselves and were not great party goers. They enjoyed each other's company and played chess most evenings. There was nothing fragile about their relationship.

It happened one evening, months after the racecourse had opened. Dorothy couldn't believe it. She thought she was dreaming and pinched herself. No, she thought. No, no no. Something must have happened to delay him. The girls were old enough now to ask questions.

"Where's Daddy? It's nearly 9 o'clock," queried Betty.

"He probably had a late meeting. I'm sure he'll be home soon," hoped Dorothy. "You girls had better get ready for bed. You've got school in the morning."

Dorothy wanted to face this on her own. She was accustomed to it. It was after 11 o'clock before Charles came home. He locked up the house but couldn't find Dorothy in the sitting room. He went into their bedroom and found Dorothy in bed, reading. He greeted her nervously "Hello love. Sorry I'm late." He didn't offer an explanation.

"Hello," said Dorothy. She slammed her book closed, turned off her bedside light and slid down under the blanket.

The next night arrived all too soon. It was 10.30 when Charles came home. She and Charles ignored each other the following morning. She was feeling devastated. Were her worst fears looming into reality? She wasn't going to allow a repeat of their weeks and weeks of silence in those dark days in Hong Kong. She decided she was going to wait up for him that night and get to the bottom of his recent late nights.

11 o'clock, then 11.30. No sign of Charles. She heard his car at 11.45. She had to confront him. She had no choice. She stood in the middle of the passage, her arms folded. She was ready for battle, or

was she? Her heart was pounding. Charles walked into the passage from the hall and he stopped in his tracks when he saw the woman he loved, poised for a fight.

"Let's go in the sitting room." She walked straight in to the sitting room and stood at the door. Charles followed her like a lamb to the slaughter. She slammed the door in an attempt to condition herself into a rage. She had to bump up her adrenalin. "What's going on?" She sounded stern, sterner than Charles had ever heard her.

"What can I say? I think you know what's happened." There was a dull tone in his voice.

"I'm not a bloody clairvoyant. Well?" She wanted to hear it from him.

"I owe money but it's not out of control."

"I knew it. I knew it would happen. It was too bloody good to be true. You were fine for over three years. It was that blasted racecourse. You've been betting, lost and now you're gambling to pay your debts, right?" Dorothy's anger had a tinge of sarcasm. She wasn't finished. "I've told you before and I'll tell you again. I do *not* have any more money to bail you out Charles. *It is finished,*" she screamed at the top of her voice. Dorothy was shaking. Not only had her temper got the better of her, she was afraid. Very afraid. She broke down and sobbed into her hands. Charles placed his hand on her shoulder to console her. She knew she had to control herself. "Leave me alone." Dorothy was swift to move away from Charles.

Charles felt empty inside as though his life, his whole world had been pulled away from under him. "Oh heavens, darling."

"Don't darling me. If you don't stop we're going to be destitute." She wanted to know how much debt he was in. She knew she couldn't help him any more. He had drained her London account. These dreadful fears added to her anger and frustration. "Let me see your recent bank statements."

"I don't know what that will achieve." He knew there were only a few pounds in the account.

"Let me see them Charles." Dorothy was not going to let up. It involved the whole family.

Charles knew he couldn't win. He went into his study, retrieved a file from a filing cabinet and returned to the sitting room. "It's getting very late. Shall we look at this tomorrow?"

Dorothy ignored him and took the file from him. She sat in a chair with the file on her lap and paged through it slowly. "Hum, at least you keep your filing up to date," snarled Dorothy. She had to remain focused, remain angry. She was thinking of their three girls and they needed educating. If Charles lost his job now they would be up the creek without a paddle. There was a lot at stake. "You've written out four cheques for quite substantial amounts recently. You had actually been saving some money Charles and it's gone, boom. Account empty. Who were the beneficiaries?" Dorothy felt like a private detective but she had no choice.

"It's all gambling related. You know that Dorothy. I just had a flutter when the racing started and it'll stop."

"It *won't* stop Charles and we both know it. You are head of this household and supposedly the breadwinner and I have never interfered with your salary or handled the family accounts. That has always been your department." Dorothy knew she had to take hold of the family finances. She continued. "I want you to ask Harvey to pay your salary in cash every month and I want you to close your bank account." Dorothy was firm and her anger had left her.

"That's ridiculous," replied Charles.

"It is not for heavens sake. We'll keep an eye on the finances together and keep the money locked away in your study. We'll keep a petty cash book of sorts. I don't want you writing out cheques willy-nilly to pay your bloody debts. You have a family to think about." Dorothy was worn out.

"We've always agreed on everything Dorothy but I draw the line there and in any event, I don't want to raise Harvey's suspicions. It's out of the question." Charles sounded determined.

"Fine. Do it your way. Carry on in your own sweet way and don't come crying to me when you get final demands and all the bloody rest of it. I've had it Charles." Dorothy stormed out of the sitting room.

The following months tested Charles and Dorothy's resolve. They muddled through each day, each week and managed to converse on daily matters. Charles was home late most evenings. Dorothy was invariably in bed and asleep when he returned home. She would receive phone calls in the evenings from men asking for Charles. It was a strain on their marriage and it was as though they had reached a stalemate. She had virtually washed her hands of his addiction. Whatever she did, it didn't help him and it was as though she was living on death row. The girls fortunately had been busy with school and their activities and they had joined the Girl Guides. Dorothy had confided in Betty and Diana as she thought them old enough to understand but they weren't able to grasp the gravity of the situation.

Dorothy was waiting for the inevitable. It happened, as she feared, at about 8 o'clock one evening. As she recalled, they had had an unwelcome visitor at their house in Hong Kong at about the same time in the evening. It seemed like a lifetime away.

A civil court official was looking for Charles to serve a summons. Dorothy was drained and at her lowest. She asked the official if she could see the summons and she scanned her eyes over the legal jargon until her eyes focused on what she had been looking for – a figure.

£2,000. She told him he would be home much later and if he wanted to return after 11 o'clock, he would probably find him at home.

That was no small amount of money. Dorothy felt sick. Sick because she no longer had financial freedom. She wasn't able to help Charles or her family and she felt like a caged animal.

Dorothy saw the summons on Charles' chest of draws in the bedroom the next morning. He had not tried to conceal it from her. She pretended she hadn't seen it. He had got himself into the mess and he could get himself out of it she thought. She knew the hearing was two days away and there was nothing, nothing she could do to help him.

The girls had just left for school and Charles and Dorothy were in the dining room. He wanted to tell her about the summons he'd received the night before. He had always meant well and was always honest with Dorothy. He trusted her explicitly and somehow he still drew strength from her. But he knew, they all knew, his addiction was a grey, secret part of his life over which he had no control.

"I received a summons last night. I have to appear in court the day after tomorrow." Charles' voice was bland.

"I know. The court official was looking for you earlier…   " Dorothy was cut short with Charles snapping at her.

"Why didn't you let me know," demanded Charles.

"For Pete's sake Charles, what a stupid comment. How the hell could I? You never tell me where you are at night, probably in some sleazy filthy bar or gambling room." Dorothy was enraged. "You can go to bloody hell." She stormed out of the dining room and into the back garden.

Charles had to appear in court. They just didn't have the finances to settle his debt. The plaintiff's lawyer and the court agreed that Charles should pay off the debt. It wasn't going to be easy and because of the size of the debt, he would have to pay almost half his monthly salary to the clerk of the civil court for over two years. It was either that or prison and if it was the latter, the plaintiff would never have seen his money.

Dorothy believed it was the beginning of the end. Although Charles was earning a good salary, halving it was going to impact on their living. They reluctantly had to release Sixpence from service. He had been with them since they arrived in Nairobi and he was a first class gardener. They were able to find other employment for him which helped Dorothy's sense of guilt. They could barely afford to keep on Girlie but she was part of the family and it would be virtually impossible asking her to leave. After paying the girls school fees and Girlie's wage, there was hardly enough left over for food. It was unsustainable.

Dorothy could turn her hand to most things. In a moment of weakness and panic she telephoned Sir Edmund and asked to see him. She didn't know who else to turn to. She arranged to meet him early one afternoon at his office at army headquarters. She walked to his office, about three miles from the house. She didn't want to tell Charles, not yet anyway, so he couldn't drive her there and the cost of a taxi was out of the question. The afternoon sun was always piercingly hot. She took shortcuts where she could, footpaths through areas of bush and her feet and shoes were full of dust by the time she arrived at headquarters feeling dirty and sweaty.

"Hello Dorothy. Come in. This is a surprise." Sir Edmund was always firm but cheerful.

"Hello Sir Edmund. Thank you for seeing me." Dorothy wanted to get to the point. "Charles will probably kill me for having seen you but my hands are tied. Charles had a civil writ against him a few weeks ago and the court instructed half his salary be paid to the plaintiff, which will take a few years to settle." Dorothy stopped for a moment.

"Dear, dear, dear. I thought Charles had stopped all that nonsense. I am sorry my dear," Sir Edmund was sincere.

"I'm not asking for any favours but I wanted to ask you if there is any work available for me in the army, in a civilian capacity of course." She stopped again and was wondering if she was doing the right thing but necessity forced her to continue. "I'm happy to do anything that's available."

"What a co-incidence. I was speaking to the quartermaster this morning and he's in need of staff – sorting out kit and that sort of thing you know. How does that sound?"

"Gosh Sir Edmund, I wasn't holding out much hope. That would be fantastic!" Dorothy was quite ecstatic.

"Leave it with me and I'll phone you in a day or two. I'm sorry about Charles. If you don't mind me saying Dorothy, he's his own worst enemy. I really thought he had overcome his problem. I'll give you a ring." Sir Edmund opened the door for Dorothy.

Dorothy didn't tell Charles of her secret meeting with Sir Edmund and would only tell him if she got the job. She was sure she would get it. She busied herself in the house and garden for the next two days. She had very mixed feelings. She wanted to be happy with the prospects of the job yet deep down she knew it was not the answer. Charles' cessation of gambling was the only long term solution to their problems. She was pleased at the thought of having her own income and she would at least be able to put a meal on the table each day. Day three dawned and Dorothy was sure she'd hear from Sir Edmund. She wanted to tell Charles about her meeting but knew she had to wait for confirmation.

Day three came and went without a call from Sir Edmund. Surely it wouldn't have taken him that long to sort out a simple job for her at the quartermaster's office? She wondered if he had forgotten. Should she phone him?

It was late afternoon on the fourth day. Dorothy was in the garden clad in a pair of long khaki shorts and a sleeveless top. Although accustomed to the heat she was perspiring from the stifling humidity compounded by her activity in the garden. Her hands and her old sandals were covered in mud from digging a new flowerbed, the muddy surrounds exacerbated by the sprinkler on the lawn. She found contentment working in the garden, surreptitiously venting her frustration and indignation on her strenuous labour.

She heard Girlie call from the house "Phone call for you Mrs Butler."

Dorothy stabbed the fork into the lawn and ran across the garden and into the house. She wiped her muddy hands on her shorts and picked up the receiver. "Hello," she said anxiously. She was quite sure it would be Sir Edmund with good news.

"Hello Dorothy." Sir Edmund's voice was bold. "I'm sorry I didn't come back to you sooner. I've been making some enquiries and I'm afraid we can't take you on."

Dorothy wanted to know every detail and quizzed him "What enquiries did you make Sir Edmund? What's wrong?"

"I can't go into detail but His Majesty's Forces can't employ staff or staff whose family or acquaintances might bring the Forces into disrepute. I'm very sorry Dorothy. I must go by the book." He sounded genuinely concerned but at the same time firm, which made Dorothy realise she had no hope in trying to convince Sir Edmund otherwise.

"Oh gosh. Oh no," said Dorothy. "I was quite sure I'd get the job. Thank you anyway Sir Edmund." She felt totally deflated and she could feel tears of frustration bubbling inside her as she replaced the receiver.

She walked slowly back to her fork in the garden, worn out and dejected. It was jutting out of the ground, lifeless, like a medieval pale through the heart of a worrier and resembling her life, broken and torn apart by the man who had brought her such love and happiness. She sat on the lawn near her excavations. The lawn was wet and she felt the moisture oozing through her shorts. She didn't care. She heard movement behind her.

"What's the matter Mummy?" It was barefooted Diana in her shorts. She picked up a loose granite stone from a nearby rockery and sat on it next to her mother.

"Oh everything darling. Don't tell Daddy but I tried to get a job the other day and it fell through." Dorothy knew she could confide in her girls.

"Why do you have to get a job?"

"You know the situation. I told you Daddy owes a lot of money. He has to pay it back and we don't have much money left over every month. We'll manage somehow. We'll have to. Now, you're filthy dirty and it's bath time now."

"Just half an hour longer Mummy. I've been in the tree house with Betty and Barbara and we're doing our homework there." Diana didn't really understand the problems that were looming ahead for the family.

"I've told you girls before, I don't want you doing home work up there. You can't write properly in there. Bath in half an hour please." Dorothy got up and got back to her flowerbed and Diana ran off towards the back of the house. Dorothy tried not to think of their problems but they were like indelible black clouds hanging over her.

Charles gave a cheque each month to the clerk of the court and brought home the balance of his salary in cash. They paid Girlie and the school in cash each month and the rest went on food. Dorothy had to cut back to stretch out their money. The girls had one glass of milk a day instead of two or three. Eggs were rationed. They had meat once a week now. It frightened Dorothy tremendously, they had never been in that situation before but she and Charles muddled through for three months. They were too distressed to discuss finances but Dorothy knew she had to talk to him. He was coming home late again and that wasn't a good sign.

It was like a repetitive nightmare. She decided to wait up for him one night but it seemed so pointless.

"Charles, we have to talk. We can barely keep our heads above water and you're gambling again, aren't you?"

"I'm only trying to get us out of this mess. I'll bring us out of it," said Charles.

"You know very well you're wasting your time *and* money. I can't take this any more. I don't want someone knocking on the door again demanding money." Dorothy had run out of energy. "Do you owe money to anyone Charles?"

"No darling. I'm managing alright," Charles lied. He had never lied to Dorothy before. He couldn't help himself and he hated doing it. "I'm being very careful and I don't want you to worry." Charles' debts were mounting again and he was desperately trying to stop spiralling into a bottomless pit.

"I don't believe you, I know you're lying. I'm telling you now Charles. We are going to end up destitute, out on the bloody street." She was feeling tearful again but she wasn't going to breakdown in front of him. She was a strong proud woman and she was annoyed that her tearfulness was becoming more and more frequent. Dorothy knew she shouldn't have broached the subject. It was always futile and left her more upset than when she started.

Dorothy had to give up her tennis and resign from the club. She couldn't afford the membership fees. She told her fellow players she had a problem with her knee and her doctor had told her to rest, unable to tell them the real reason.

She had been doing a lot of sewing, making dresses and shorts for the girls. They lived in shorts and were little tomboys. Dorothy was at her machine one night burning the midnight oil and there was still no sign of Charles. It was four months since he had appeared in court and he had been coming home late most nights but he was always home before midnight. It became part of Dorothy's roller coaster life and it was taking a toll on her health. She was run down and losing weight. She had notable bags under her eyes and she knew she felt and looked a wreck.

It was 12.15am when Dorothy went to bed. She dozed on and off and she felt exhausted when the alarm clock went off at 5.45. Charles' side of the bed was neat and tidy. She knew he hadn't come home, as she had been awake more than she had dozed. She felt sick in the stomach. Now she was worried and wondered if he had been involved in an accident. She tried to dispel that; she was sure the police would have notified her.

She decided to phone the hospital anyway. She slipped on her shorts and a cotton shirt and ran barefoot through to Charles' study and dialled the hospital casualty. There was only one government hospital in the town. She gave them his name and told them of her concern but they assured her he hadn't been admitted.

Where the hell was he, she thought to herself. She would phone the police. They would know if anything had happened. She phoned the central charge office and told the Sergeant he had not come home last night and asked if there had been any reports of an accident or some mishap. The Sergeant asked her to hold on. Dorothy was standing next to the desk in Charles' study, tapping a brass container with a pencil.

"Hello," came the Sergeants voice down the phone. "We have a man by that name detained here."

"What do you mean detained? What has happened?" queried Dorothy.

"Detained in our cells ma'am but I'm not allowed to supply information over the phone. You'll have to come down to the charge office for any information." The Sergeant sounded formal.

"Thank you." Dorothy put the phone down. "Oh shit," she said quietly to herself and as she turned around she saw Betty, Diana and Barbara standing in the doorway of the study. They were in their blue and white polka-dot school uniforms, white ankle socks and brown shoes. They appeared dejected, frightened, distinctly fragile. The girls were losing weight, they looked emaciated, their thin little arms and legs dangling like feeble sticks from their uniforms. "Oh my darlings." She held her girls in her arms and hugged them, devastated and suddenly aware of their desperate situation. They responded in a silent embrace, their arms around her like an entangled octopus.

Barbara spoke first "What's wrong Mummy?"

"Where's Daddy?" Betty asked.

"Daddy's at the police station." Dorothy wanted to be honest with them but didn't say he was in jail. She wanted confirmation of that. "I'm going down there now. You all get off to school and I'll see you this afternoon."

"Is he in jail?" Betty asked. They all knew their father had been in court before and owned money to someone.

"I bet he is," said Diana.

"Just keep this under your hats please, as you always have. It's a family problem and we'll sort it out. Now, *off* you go, go on. School!" Dorothy hugged her girls again. Somehow they gave her confidence and she was glad she could talk to them.

Dorothy dressed and made herself respectable. She rushed back into the study and phoned for a taxi. The police station was on the other side of the town and she didn't want to waste time walking there.

The taxi stopped outside the charge office. It cost her a fortune, so she thought, and the money could have been better spent feeding the girls. She walked up the steps and to the wooden counter. A Sergeant approached her and she spoke to him.

"I phoned here earlier and I understand Charles Butler has been detained. Can you tell me what has happened?"

"Are you related to him ma'am?" Dorothy recognised the Sergeant's voice from her earlier call.

"Well, yes." Dorothy hesitated for a moment. "He's my husband. Can you tell me why he's detained please?" Dorothy spoke quietly and decisively.

"We had a complaint of fraud ma'am. He made out a cheque to someone and the bank was unable to honour it. He had insufficient funds in his account." The Sergeant had a folder on the counter in front of him.

"What happens now?" asked Dorothy.

"He'll be taken before a magistrate this morning. He'll be given the opportunity to plead guilty or not guilty. The magistrate will decide whether to sentence him or remand the case. I'm sorry ma'am." The Sergeant noticed Dorothy's anguish.

"I don't believe this." Dorothy held her head down. "Can I see him?"

"Not now, but he'll be taken to the courts shortly and you can see him there." As the Sergeant spoke she saw Charles being led along a corridor towards the charge office. She couldn't believe what she saw. He was barefoot, his hair was dishevelled and he had dark stubble on his face. He was led into a room before reaching the charge office. Dorothy waited at the counter. He had to come out. She was right. He had his shoes on now but his hair was still a mess and he was unshaven. His smart blazer with brass buttons and his old regimental badge on the pocket, check shirt and bow tie looked incongruous. A Sergeant and Constable led him into the charge office and he saw Dorothy and stopped. Their eyes met and mirrored their mutual feelings of deep depression and helplessness. Neither of them spoke and the police officers sensed their passion and desperation. They led him passed Dorothy to a waiting police truck outside.

The Sergeant behind the counter broke the silence. "The magistrates court is a ten minute walk from here ma'am, on the corner of...   "

Dorothy interrupted him. "Yes, I know. Thank you." Her voice was shaking. She walked to the court and tried to shake off her depression. A car pulled up alongside her and an elderly woman offered her a lift but she declined, wanting to be on her own to think.

She saw the cream coloured two storey building ahead, the main entrance evidenced by the Union Jack and a coat of arms above the double wooden doors. She didn't hesitate climbing the wide sweeping steps into the building.

The walk had done her good and she felt a bit better. She walked along the corridor and saw a sign marked 'Prosecutors Office' above a doorway. A good a place as any, thought Dorothy. She went into the office and asked a young woman if she knew of Charles' case. The woman took a sheet of paper from a wire filing basket on her desk, indicating his name was on the court roll in court number two.

The courtroom was massive with wooden panelled walls. The prisoner's dock stood ominously in the centre of the courtroom with the magistrate's bench at the front of the court with a high-backed maroon coloured leather chair. A row of tables for use by the prosecutor and defence council separated the bench and the dock. Several wooden benches were placed neatly at the back of the court and Dorothy sat down. She felt anxious and uncomfortable. A policeman paced the courtroom with a pen in one hand and piece of paper in the other.

A tall scrawny individual clutching a pile of folders swept passed her and into the courtroom, his long black gown flowing precariously behind him. The room was buzzing with activity and a loud knock on the door behind the magistrate's bench brought the court to order.

The man in black bellowed out loudly. "Silence in court."

The door opened and a venerable looking character displaying bushy white sideburns and an unruly shaggy moustache of similar shade, glided into the courtroom and flung his black gown into the air behind him as he sat down behind the bench. Dorothy wondered where Charles was.

"Case one on the roll your Worship. It is requested the accused be further remanded in custody for a week," requested the prosecutor.

"Well where is the prisoner Mr Prosecutor?" The magistrate was abrupt.

The prosecutor looked behind him and went bright red. The prisoner's dock was empty.

"I'm sorry your Worship. Bear with me." The prosecutor peered down the stairs in the prisoner's dock. "Warder, can we have the prisoner for case one," shouted the prosecutor. The prisoner appeared a second later and was pushed up the stairs by a prison warder behind him. The prisoner stood in the dock with the warder next to him.

"Why a further remand?" The magistrate was addressing the prosecutor.

"The police require more time to investigate the case. They feel the prisoner may interfere with witnesses and request he be remanded in custody your Worship."

"Right, right." The magistrate looked at the prisoner and asked his name.

"You are remanded until 14th of this month in this court," The magistrate was looking at the prisoner in the dock. "Next," snapped the magistrate.

"Case two your Worship. This matter may be for plea or remand." The prosecutor looked down the stairs into the holding cells and saw Charles climbing the stairs. He stood in the prisoners dock with a warder next to him. "Allow me to approach the prisoner your Worship." The prosecutor turned to Charles. "How do you plead to the charge of fraud against you?"

"Well, I'm not sure." Charles was nervous.

"Did you issue a cheque with insufficient funds to meet it?" asked the prosecutor.

"Yes sir," replied Charles.

"You have the opportunity to plead guilty or not guilty. If you wish you may appoint a lawyer to act on your behalf," explained the prosecutor.

"No, I just want to get it over with please," answered Charles.

"Your Worship, the accused wishes to plead guilty to the charge of fraud. May I read the indictment to him?"

"Yes, yes Mr Prosecutor. Get on with it." The magistrate was frustrated at the delay.

The prosecutor read the charge to Charles. It was quite audible at the back of the court and Dorothy could hear everything. Charles had fraudulently issued a cheque for £3,000 to a man named in the indictment, knowing he did not have the funds to meet it.

"How do you plead?"

"Guilty sir." Charles answered quietly.

"How much is in your account?" the magistrate asked Charles.

"About £10 sir," answered Charles.

"What is your monthly salary?" the magistrate continued to quiz Charles.

"£200 a month sir."

"Why did you issue the cheque knowing it wouldn't be honoured by your bank?" asked the magistrate.

"The complainant kept asking me for the money and I gave him the cheque to stop him worrying me," explained Charles

"Did you know it was wrong, that it was fraud?" asked the magistrate.

"Yes sir. It was a stupid decision on my part. I'm sorry," answered Charles.

"Anything else Mr Prosecutor?" asked the magistrate.

"No your Worship."

"This court finds you guilty as charged. The court will take into account your co-operation with the police and this court when passing sentence. Any previous convictions Mr Prosecutor?" asked the magistrate.

"I'd like to ask for a weeks remand to allow police to check for previous convictions your Worship. I have no objection to the accused being remanded out of custody but in view of the amount involved, it is requested the accused surrender his passport to the clerk of court and report once a day to the police," requested the prosecutor.

"Charles Butler. You are remanded to the 14th of this month in this court for sentence. You are to surrender your passport to the clerk of the court by 4 o'clock today and report to the police once a day, commencing tomorrow," explained the magistrate.

Do you understand?"

"Yes sir," answered Charles. The prison warder opened the dock door and allowed Charles out. He was free to go for the time being. He walked to be back of the court and saw Dorothy. She got up and walked out of the court with him. Both were silent. They walked to the entrance of the courts and stood at the top of the steps in the sun.

"Where's your car?" asked Dorothy bluntly.

"At the office," said Charles.

"Where did the police arrest you?" Dorothy's voice had no tone.

"At the office," said Charles.

"So Harvey knows about this?" asked Dorothy.

"Yes," replied Charles.

They were both nervous and embarrassed at their new experience and just got on with the basics.

"The office is a ten minute walk from here. I want to see Harvey and gauge his reaction." Charles was to the point. "I'll have to get my passport here this afternoon."

They walked to Charles' office in silence. It was nearly 10 o'clock and the sun was burning already. The town was alive with cars, cyclists and pedestrians. They reached the office and Charles suggested Dorothy waited outside. She stood in the shade of a tree in the car park near the office.

Charles went straight to Harvey's office and knocked on the door. He knew he had to get it over with eventually. It's now or never he thought.

"Come in." He heard Harvey's voice.

Charles tried to smooth his hair with his hands. "Oh damn it," he said to himself having remembered he hadn't shaved. "Shit," he said out loud. "Too late." He opened Harvey's door and braced himself. "Good morning sir."

Harvey had a sullen face. He glanced at Charles, got up from his desk and stood at the window with his back to him. His fists rested on a table under the window, his knuckles taut. The silence was deafening.

"Sir," Charles cleared his throat nervously, "I must apologise for what happened yesterday."

Harvey remained silent. He was thinking. Charles was an exceptionally good engineer and he got on with him. Nairobi was a small town and rumours spread like wild fire. If he retained Charles, it would not do the company image any good. An engineer with a criminal record, and fraud at that. Harvey was weighing all the pros and cons.

Harvey broke the icy silence. "Charles, I'm the managing director of this company. The chairman and directors are based in London as you know." He still had his back to Charles. He felt an element of remorse but his hands were tied. "I have no alternative but to inform the board and they would expect me to take the necessary action. I'm sorry Charles."

"What are you saying, sir?" Charles couldn't come to grips with it.

"You know damn well what I'm saying. Do I have to spell it out for you?" It was clear Harvey regretted his decision.

"Could I not be given a warning sir?" Charles was desperate.

"It's no good Charles." Harvey plucked up the courage to turn around. "The company's reputation is at stake. Fraud is not to be taken lightly. It's a crime of dishonesty. Your dismissal takes effect from today. My hands are tied." Harvey walked around his desk and opened the door. "Please leave the car keys with my secretary. I'll write to you regarding the house and your final salary."

Charles left the office and made no further comment. He walked out of the building and saw Dorothy waiting under the tree. His throat was tight and he felt light headed.

"Let's walk back to the house," said Charles.

"Where's the car?" Dorothy feared the worst.

Charles didn't answer and they started walking along the pavement.

"Well?" asked Dorothy.

"I've been fired." Charles had said it. He felt his head spinning and he was sweating.

He couldn't think straight. He was cursing himself in his mind.

Dorothy didn't answer. She knew disaster had struck. She feared it all those years ago in India, then Ceylon and then Hong Kong. Their life, as they knew it, had been whipped from under their feet. She felt as though her soul had been torn apart by a pride of marauding lions.

Girlie was in the kitchen when they arrived home. Dorothy made a pot of tea and sat at the table in the kitchen. She poured two cups. "Please give that to Mr Butler, wherever he is." Dorothy sounded exhausted. She lit a cigarette and exhaled the smoke forcefully in front of her. Only her second one today she thought. She had managed to cut down. She stared blankly at the kitchen cupboard, her elbows on the table and held the teacup in both hands.

Charles stood at the kitchen door. "I'm taking my passport down to the court."

Dorothy ignored him and sipped her tea. Girlie was preparing vegetables at the sink.

"What's wrong Mrs Butler?" Girlie was concerned. She never asked questions but she knew something was seriously wrong.

"Mr Butler has lost his job Girlie." She had known her long enough to be honest with her. "The police arrested him yesterday for fraud. He wrote out a cheque for someone, which he knew he couldn't honour. It's all a crazy nightmare." Her safety valve gave way and she started crying.

"Oh no, Mrs Butler." Girlie sat in the empty chair next to Dorothy and put her arm around her shoulder. "I would never have thought he would do that."

"Neither did I," said Dorothy. She reached for a tissue in her pocket and blew her nose. It sounded like a foghorn.

"What will happen now?" queried Girlie.

"I have no idea. I really, really have no idea Girlie. I don't want to think about it." Dorothy covered her face with her hands.

Charles received a letter a few days later from Harvey. They had to vacate their company house in six weeks, by 31ˢᵗ March. He felt a sense of relief as he read the letter but it only lasted a few seconds. What then he asked himself. Everything was coming to a head. He owed around £5,000. Charles sat at his desk in his study his thoughts turbulent, muddled. He knew he couldn't pay that, not now. He had to think straight. He had to appear in court in a few days for sentence on the fraud charge. Would he be given time to pay he thought. How could he pay? He had better look for new employment. Nothing was falling into place. There was one huge insurmountable hurdle after another.

"Silence in court," blurted the prosecutor, which summonsed the magistrate into the courtroom. "Your Worship, can we attend to the first case on the roll."

A policeman was standing near the prisoner's dock and made the ritual triple call for the accused. "Charles Butler, Charles Butler, Charles Butler."

Charles was sitting at the back of the court with Dorothy. He stood up and walked uncertainly towards the dock.

"Stand in the dock," said the policeman.

"State your full names," said the prosecutor.

"Charles Butler sir," said Charles.

"Your Worship. The accused has no previous convictions for fraud or dishonesty," said the prosecutor. "It is requested the court passes sentence."

The magistrate wriggled in his chair and cleared his throat. "This is a serious case before the court. The court has accepted your plea of guilty. You wilfully, unlawfully and with fraudulent intent issued a cheque for £3,000 to the complainant. He presented it to the bank but your bank was not able to honour the payment as you had insufficient funds in your account. On your own admission you have a mere £10 in your account and earn £200 a month. Clearly you had no intention of paying the complainant. The court views this very seriously. Do you have anything to say in mitigation before I pass sentence?"

Charles stood up in the dock. His family and life were on the line. "Your Worship," said Charles, mimicking the prosecutor's court lingo. "I lost my job last week because of this case. I owe the clerk of the civil court about £2000 in another case. I would like the opportunity to seek new employment so I can settle these debts. My family and I have to be out of our company house at the end of March." Charles stopped for a moment and coughed nervously. His voice was shaking. "I'm asking the court to be lenient with me and allow me to look after my family. That is all."

The magistrate wrote down Charles' mitigation in a barely legible scrawl.

"You say you owe nearly £2000 in a civil suit. This court has no jurisdiction over civil matters but has taken cognisance of your admission." The magistrate stopped briefly, looking back through his notes. He cleared his throat again and looked directly at Charles. "This court takes into account your co-operation with the police and the court. You have committed a serious offence and the amount involved is quite substantial. You should have thought about your family before getting yourself into debt and the consequences of this crime. You have been a menace to society and it is hoped your sentence will put you on the right path." The magistrate stopped again momentarily and fidgeted with the papers before him. "This court sentences you to 12 months imprisonment with hard labour, 6 months of which is suspended for 3 years on condition you do not commit a crime of dishonesty within those 3 years. Do you understand?"

"Yes sir." Charles felt like a caged animal. There was little he could say or do.

The prison warder standing outside the dock moved swiftly. He entered the dock and took Charles by the upper arm. "Down to the holding cells," said the warder.

"Can I speak to my wife?" asked Charles.

"No," snapped the warder. "There are visiting hours at the prison."

Charles started his descent into the cells under the court. He turned his head as he disappeared into the pits of hell and just caught a glimpse of Dorothy standing alone and anxious at the back of the court. His heart pounded. His sorrow was indescribable and he wanted to hold and be with the woman he loved so much.

Dorothy had a feeling of utter despair. She was looking for support but court officials ignored her. They were accustomed to this sort of thing every day. She wanted to speak to Charles and managed to attract the attention of the prison warder in the courtroom. He came over to her and he explained she could only see him at the prison between 10am and 12pm and 3pm and 5pm each day. She left the court and wasted no time getting home.

Fortunately the girls were still at school. She had some very hard decisions to make and needed Girlie's support. "Girlie, come and sit with me." She was hanging out the washing in the back garden and came in quickly to be with Dorothy. "Girlie I have to be level headed for the girls. Now listen. Mr Butler has been sent to prison for 6 months…"

Girlie interrupted but was hardly surprised. "Oh no, Mrs Butler."

Dorothy contained herself. "We have to be out of this house in five weeks. We have no money and no income now. I just don't know where we'll go. Girlie, I hate to have to say this, but I won't be able to employ you from next week. I'll help you find a new job."

"Mrs Butler, I knew all this would happen and I think you did too but perhaps you couldn't accept it or believe it. I was able to look at it from the outside. I made some enquiries on my own last week. Can I tell you?"

"What have you been up to?" There was a sound of hope in Dorothy's voice. "Shall we have a cup of tea? Perhaps we need something stronger!" giggled Dorothy. She scratched in her bag for a cigarette and lit up. "What enquiries did you make?"

Girlie turned on the kettle. "I've been speaking to a farmer at Max's grocery store for the last few weeks. She shops there frequently. She told me her maid is pregnant and wants to return to her rural home and she asked me to look for a maid for her."

"How long have you known her?" asked Dorothy.

"Oh, I've seen her many times and we always greet each other and chat. Her name is Mrs Jenkins. Do you know her?" quizzed Girlie as she poured the water in the teapot. She went on. "Anyway, I told her yesterday that I might be available, but Mrs Butler, I'll only leave when you're ready."

"Don't be silly Girlie. You have your life to think about. As we're talking, I'm wondering if this Mrs Jenkins might have a little cottage, even a cow shed, for me and the girls on her farm." Dorothy joked at her latter suggestion but deep down she was panicking.

"Are you serious?" asked Girlie.

"Girlie I couldn't be more serious. I have to find somewhere to live. And to top it all, I can't afford to pay rent. I just don't believe this."

"Would you like me to ask her if she has anywhere for you to stay?" asked Girlie.

"Yes, of course. Will you be able to see her today?" Dorothy was desperate.

"I'll go to Max's at 3 o'clock. She's usually there mid afternoon," promised Girlie.

It was a week since Charles received his sentence. Dorothy hadn't been to see him in prison. She didn't want to see him in there, talking to him behind bars. She had so much to think about she didn't know if she was coming or going. Girlie had managed to see Mrs Jenkins at Max's last week and she arranged with Girlie that she'd call on Dorothy at 12 noon today.

Dorothy spent a lot of time with Girlie who was always positive and gave her support.

"I hope Mrs Jenkins hasn't forgotten." Dorothy looked at the clock on the kitchen wall. It was 12.20pm and as she spoke they heard a vehicle at the front of the house. "Come with me," said Dorothy and took Girlie by the hand. They reached the hallway and saw a short plump woman on the veranda. She wore a dirty torn pair of khaki shorts and a khaki shirt in equally poor state of repair with epaulettes and two pockets on the chest. An old cracked leather belt was pulled tightly around her waist, seemingly having the purpose of not only holding up her shorts but pulling in an extended belly as well. She had an old pair of sandals on her dusty feet with toenails that were in need of a farrier's hoof rasp.

"Hello, I'm Dorothy Butler."

"Hello, I'm Esther Jenkins." The round woman had an accent Dorothy couldn't quite detect. She held out her hand and shook Dorothy's hand vigorously.

Dorothy felt like a fool now asking this strange woman for accommodation but she knew she had no choice. "I believe you might have somewhere for us to stay?" asked Dorothy.

The plump woman wasted no time. "I have two old but well built grass huts on the farm. They were part of the original farmhouse. You're welcome to have a look at them."

Dorothy couldn't say no. "Do you have time to show us now?"

"Of course. We're about 5 miles from here. I'll give you direction."

"Um, I don't have a car. Could you take us there please?" Dorothy hated being dependent on anyone.

"Jump in," said Esther and walked to her Ford truck.

Dorothy locked the house and she and Girlie squeezed into the cab of the one-ton truck. Esther walked to the front of the truck and cranked the engine. The engine splattered and the truck rattled into life.

They drove out of Nairobi town and turned off onto a bush road. The truck shuddered over the rough track. After a mile or so, they turned on to narrow dusty strips, with long brown elephant grass on either side. The truck bulldozed the grass in the middle of the strips as Esther sped towards a dwelling house. She drove a few hundred yards behind it and stopped the truck in a cloud of dust outside two grass huts.

"Here we are," said Esther. "We used to store drums of molasses in them until we built those barns over there." Esther pointed to a group of buildings a distance away. "Have a look." She clambered out of the truck and opened the door of one hut and went in.

Dorothy and Girlie followed in silence. They knew what each other were thinking. Basic wasn't the word. It was a small room, barely 30 feet square with a door and a window. The other hut, right next door, was exactly the same. They were made of thatched grass and a mixture of dried mud and cement were used to plaster the floor and walls. An old wooden framed window had four filthy windowpanes in it. The hut smelt musty and was quite dark inside.

Esther spoke. "Girlie told me you needed somewhere to stay where you didn't have to pay rent. It's none of my business but can I ask why you want to do this?" Esther was quite forthright.

Dorothy had to be straight with her. "My husband has a serious problem with gambling. It's an addiction. He borrowed some money from someone and gave him a cheque he couldn't honour. He's lost his job and is serving 6 months now." Dorothy felt as though she was dreaming. It was an unbelievable nightmare. "We have to be out of the company house by the end March."

"You're welcome to use these huts. You won't have to pay rent but you'll have to be self sufficient." Esther was disinterested with Dorothy's horror story and offered no words of sympathy. "Oh, the toilet is behind the huts. It's only a long drop but it'll do."

"Long drop?" queried Dorothy.

"Yes. Come I'll show you." Esther showed her a small grass hut. It had a rickety wooden door about to fall off its hinge and it creaked as she opened it. "There," she said.

Dorothy peered cautiously inside. There was a large wooden box-like structure about knee height with a hole in it. "Oh," said Dorothy. "Is *that* the toilet?" she asked unbelievingly.

"Yes. The hole below the seat is 15 feet deep. It's quite adequate," said Esther, unconcerned

Good grief, Dorothy thought to herself. "Thank you," Dorothy said politely. It was the last place on earth she wanted. She wanted to run away from the place, run as fast as she could but she had to accept it as a new home for her and the girls. "I believe you may want to employ Girlie?" Dorothy changed the subject.

"Yes. I'll show you your accommodation." Esther was a woman of few words. There was a long building about 50 yards from the barns. They consisted of staff rooms, toilets, showers and a kitchen. It was not what Girlie had been accustomed to but it was a roof over her head and a job. "Everybody happy?" asked Esther. "I'll probably see Girlie at Max's and she can tell me when you're ready to move."

CHAPTER 5

D orothy had to clear out the house and sell most of their belongings. There was only room for one single bed in each hut and a couple of chairs. She would take her carpets and a few pots and pans. There was just no room for anything. Dorothy placed an advert. in Max's window. They had a steady stream of buyers over a week and she managed to sell everything that needed selling. The money she had from the sale of the furniture and their bits and pieces would help feed them for a few months she thought. She was worn out mentally and physically. The thought of those huts being her new home was taking its toll on her morale. The end of the school term was drawing near and Dorothy had told the girls that they would have to leave school. She just didn't have the money for their school fees.

The 31st March arrived. Girlie had arranged for Esther to collect them with their goods and chattels. Betty, Diana and Barbara were very quiet as was Dorothy and Girlie. Their beds, chairs, carpets, suitcases and cardboard boxes were on the veranda. The house was empty.

A strange car arrived in the driveway. A man got out and approached Dorothy.

"Hello. Mr Harvey has asked me to collect the keys to the house," said the strange man.

"Oh, of course," said Dorothy. She had forgotten the phone call from Harvey earlier in the week. "Would you like to go over the house with me?" she asked politely.

"Yes, why not," said Harvey's factotum.

Dorothy entered each room systematically. She also wanted to be sure they had not left anything behind. The girls and Girlie had done a superb job cleaning the empty rooms. Their footsteps on the wooden strip floorboards echoed in the rooms and gave an eerie, lonely feeling. They went back onto the veranda and Dorothy handed the man the house keys and allowed him to lock the front door.

"Thank you," he said and left hastily for his car.

The front garden was like a bus station. He had no sooner left when Esther drove in to the garden in her dented, dusty rattletrap. Her Ford was relatively new but had become a workhorse on her farm and its hard life was starting to show signs of wear and tear.

"Everyone ready I see," said Esther. She opened the tailgate at the back of the truck. "Now, can we get the beds in first." The woman of few words didn't greet them.

It took them a good half hour to load the truck. They planned it to enable the girls to have a place to sit. It was piled high and Dorothy had wisely kept some rope from the garden shed, in anticipation of having to tie everything down. The garden fork, spade and an old hosepipe were the last things to go in and they had difficulty finding a place to put them. Dorothy and Girlie sat in the cab and the girls sat huddled in the little holes they had reserved amongst their tangled belongings, all they had left of their shredded lives. The girls hadn't seen their new abode and had relied on Dorothy's description. They weren't looking forward to it.

It was nearly midday by the time they had unloaded the truck.

Esther drove off having said little to them. The five of them stood next to their furniture. They had hardly spoken all day.

"Mummy we can't stay here," said Betty and Barbara agreed. They looked inside the huts. "It's terrible."

"It's the best Mummy can do for us. Anyway, it's all Daddy's fault." Diana sounded supportive. "Let's put the carpets inside then they'll look better."

It was a case of a square peg in a round hole but they manoeuvred and folded the carpets until the floors were totally covered. It looked better already. Then the beds went in, then a chest of drawers and a table in each hut. Dorothy kept the old kitchen curtains and they fitted with a few adjustments.

"I think they look very nice now." Dorothy tried to convince the girls. "What do you think?"

Diana was still positive. "They're all right Mummy. It's not your fault."

"Now girls. How about putting your Girl Guide knowledge to work!" Dorothy wanted to make light of everything. "Let's make a fire and have a cup of tea." There was a large acacia tree near the huts and Esther had told them to make use of a pile of cut wood under the tree. Barbara gathered some big granite stones lying around the area.

"Let's make the fire around the back of the huts then the smoke won't go in the doors," suggested Betty.

They made a neat cooking area with the stones. An old piece of wire gauze leaning up against the barn was ideal for placing over the fire. In no time Diana had raging flames and added pieces of wood to it and the kettle was filled from a nearby standpipe. Luckily they brought five canvas deck chairs and they placed them under the acacia tree. The pantry consisted of three large cardboard boxes and Dorothy scratched around for the tea, sugar and powdered milk.

89

Tea poured, Dorothy collapsed in a deck chair and sipped the tea. "Hmm, it tastes different, nicely different."

"Anything cooked on a fire tastes different, even stews or vegetables," said Diana. They had learnt some bush craft as Girl Guides and Diana was a particularly good cook. "We've got a bit of meat from the house. I'll cook it for supper tonight before it goes off."

They all had their tea. Betty, Diana and Barbara went for a walk to familiarise themselves with the area. Dorothy poured herself another cup of tea. She hadn't had a cigarette all day and she was dying for one. She took the box from her shorts pocket but it barely resembled a box. The cigarettes had been squashed but were still intact. She poked a dry piece of elephant grass on the embers and it ignited into a flame. She lit her cigarette and threw the burning grass onto the fire. She sat back in her chair and pulled heavily on her cigarette. She closed her eyes and felt unexpectedly at peace. Perhaps she had resigned herself to this very unusual situation they were in. She drew on her cigarette and sipped her smoky flavoured tea. Her feeling of peace slowly melted and was replaced with fear, almost panic that welled up inside her. The money she had would last about two months she thought. All they had to buy was food and she had to be very conservative with it.

"Mummy," called Diana. "We remembered a Girl Guide trick. If Mrs Jenkins can let us have some thin wire gauze, we can make a fridge."

"That sounds funny. How will you do that?"

"We'll show you."

Diana was preparing their first meal in the bush. She cut the meat into squares and diced an onion. The fat from the meat was sizzling in a black enamel pot on the fire. The cooking oil ran out weeks ago and was regarded a 'luxury' in their household. She put the onion and meat into the rendered fat and stirred it. She allowed it to brown then added some water and popped the lid on the pot. She washed some cabbage leaves and left them on the table under the tree. It was getting dark but her eyes adjusted as dusk slipped into darkness.

She sat in a chair by the fire. The other three were also sitting near the fire, gazing silently at the embers. A gust of wind blew and sparks and smoke flew into the air then settled down again.

"How long will we be here?" asked Barbara.

"I don't know darling. We're very lucky Mrs Jenkins has allowed us to stay here. Daddy won't be out of jail for three or four months," said Dorothy.

"What will happen when he comes out?" quizzed Barbara again.

"We'll have to wait and see but for now we'll have to take each day as it comes." Dorothy tried to sound positive for the girls but felt emptiness inside. "How are you doing with the supper darling?" Dorothy asked Diana.

Diana poked the meat in the pot then put the mound of cabbage leaves in the juice in the pot. "Another ten minutes and we can eat," she said.

Dorothy found the plates in a cardboard box and stacked them on the table with the knives and forks. Diana took the big black pot to the table and spooned out the stew equally onto the four waiting plates. "There you are. Eat up before it gets cold." Diana took a plate and knife and fork to her mother, then got her own. Betty and Barbara helped themselves.

"Hmmm. Bon appetit," said Dorothy.

"What?" asked Betty.

"Nothing."

Their first meal was surprisingly good and as Diana had rightly said, it had a special flavour, a smoky campfire taste. Although they were still hungry, there were no second helpings. They were used to that. It was nearly 9 o'clock by the time they'd washed the dishes and put everything away. Their whole routine was different and everything a challenge. Washing the dishes was a challenge. They had to heat the water on the fire, then take it to a bowl on the table. There was nowhere to bath, not even a shower. Esther had not allowed them to use the staff ablutions. The girls had found an old but clean five-gallon tin near the barn and that was all they could use to wash themselves. Sleeping arrangements had been sorted out. Betty and Barbara were to share one bed and Dorothy and Diana the other.

"I think we had better get to bed. It's been a long day," said Dorothy. She kissed and hugged Betty and Barbara and ensured they were safely in their hut then joined Diana. It was strange, all so strange. Dorothy lay awake for hours with so much churning over in her thoughts. Charles had been in prison for six weeks and she hadn't been to see him. It wasn't that she didn't love him. She knew it would upset her. But she had had so much on her plate, selling up, deciding what to keep, what to sell, consoling the girls, visiting their headmistress at the school. It was endless. Their future, especially the uncertainty, made her stomach turn.

Three days passed. Dorothy was thinking more and more about Charles, now that she had little to do. It was a long way in to town but the girls had found out that local buses used the main road quite frequently. She had to see him and tell him what was happening.

She told the girls to remain on the farm and she left early in the morning and started the two mile hike to the main road. There were no bus stops. It was rural Africa and she just hoped a bus would pass. It was a good three miles into town and she decided to start walking. There was bush on either side of the road and she could see the odd homestead in the distance. It was spring and the grass and bush were brown after a dry winter. The rains fell in summer in Kenya, between April and August. Wild game was not uncommon on the outskirts of Nairobi, although buck, warthog and the like were the most common. Dorothy hoped she wouldn't encounter a hyena or even worse, a lion. The bush along the edge of the road was thick in places and she peered into it hoping not to see any movement. She had walked for about ten minutes on the main road and was beginning to think she was stupid walking on her own, when she heard the rumble of a vehicle in the distance. She looked back and saw a car approaching. She continued walking but decided to wave it down. Dorothy realised she might be lucky when she heard the car slowing down. It stopped next to her and the middle-aged man in a suit asked her if she wanted a lift. She was grateful for the offer and he dropped her in the centre of Nairobi. She had no idea where the prison was and she wasn't going to ask the man in the suit.

That wasn't too bad she thought. She stood outside the town hall. Who could she ask for directions to the prison? She didn't fancy asking anyone such a question. She had a brainwave, she'd ask at the Magistrate's court. Dorothy was given concise directions and found out it was not far from the road leading out to the farm. It would be easier for her next visit. She had plenty of time before visiting hour at 10 o'clock and she strolled in the direction of the prison.

A large high white wall topped with barbed wire loomed ahead of her. Sentry towers were on the two corners she could see from the road. Massive medieval looking wooden doors with a small pedestrian door within it seemed to be the only access to the prison. About twelve people had gathered outside the closed doors and Dorothy joined them. A prisoner warder opened the small door and they were allowed in after giving the name of the prisoner they were visiting. Dorothy's turn came.

"I've come to see Charles Butler."

The warder summonsed her in. She stood in a small courtyard with the other visitors. The warder locked the door with a mass of keys on a large metal ring. He walked into an office and everyone followed, clearly accustomed to the routine. They followed him down a long narrow passage with prison bars along its length that looked out onto a small courtyard. A few minutes later, men clad in long white shorts and baggy shirts filed into the courtyard and they greeted their visitors through the bars. There was no sign of Charles. She peered anxiously at the door the men had come through. Then a man appeared at the door and stood in the courtyard. She wasn't sure if it was Charles. He looked drawn and skeletal with a shaved head. His shoulders were rounded like a broken man and he was barefoot. His eyes were sunken as were his cheeks and he stared blankly at the visitors. It *was* him she thought.

"Charles," she whispered loudly.

He ignored her and stood still with a blank gaze.

"Charles!" Dorothy called out.

He moved his head and looked towards Dorothy.

"Charles," she called again and waved her arm through the bars.

Charles' expression changed for a moment from blank to confused then he ran towards Dorothy with short uncertain steps, his bare feet scuffing the stone floor. He put both arms through the bars and squeezed her like an orang-utan. He held her so tightly against the bars she could hardly breathe and the side of her face was squashed into the iron that separated them.

"Charles darling, I can't breathe!" she joked.

"My sweet, where have you been? Oh how I've missed you. I've been so worried about you." He was sobbing like a child.

They talked and talked for two hours and the time flew by. Dorothy walked out of the wooden door of the prison. The midday sun was beating down and she took a floppy khaki hat and a pair of sunglasses out of her bag and decided to go straight back to the farm but stopped at a small grocery store. They had no food at the huts other than the remains of a cabbage. Maize meal goes a long way she thought. It was ground maize and cooked up like porridge. It was nutritious and was served with meat and gravy and vegetables. The little butchery in the store was selling soup bones at a special price. She couldn't resist them. What about a loaf of bread? Yes she thought. She'd spoil them. She reached the main road and started walking in the direction of the farm, hoping again for a lift or a rural bus the girls had spoken about. The sun was burning her bare arms. A few cars passed but didn't stop. She heard the sound of a vehicle behind her. Good, she thought. It was a bus. Dorothy waved it down and it stopped for her. The roof looked like a junkyard with chairs, bags of food, ploughs, wheelbarrows and other paraphernalia. The bus was packed with passengers. She told the driver she wanted to travel for about three miles and she would tell him where to stop.

She stood near the front of the bus next to a wizened old woman in an isle seat. She had a beehive shaped basket on her lap and Dorothy noticed it was full of chirping chicks.

That's a good idea she thought. The woman spoke broken English and after a little sales talk agreed to sell four to Dorothy. She put them in her hat attracting laughter from the other passengers. The bus neared the turn off to the farm and Dorothy tapped the driver on the shoulder. She walked along the dusty road to the farm hoping her money was well spent. Her arms were full with her purchases and the five pound bag of maize meal.

"Hello everyone." Dorothy heard hammering behind the huts. Diana was hammering thin wire gauze onto a wooden frame. Five other gauzed frames lay next to her. "What are you up to?"

"We're making a fridge," said Diana.

"We learnt how to make them in Girl Guides," added Barbara. "Just as well we brought Daddy's tool box. We've used the hammer and saw and used some nails."

"Where did you get the gauze and wood?"

"We asked Mrs Jenkins. It's old mosquito gauze she'd used on windows and doors. Did you see Daddy?" Diana didn't stop her hammering.

"Well I'm confused. You'll have to show me how it works. Yes, he's fine and was very happy to see me. He's lost a lot of weight though," said Dorothy.

"We all have," said Betty. "Something's moving in your hat!" she exclaimed.

"I bought these from a woman on the bus. Look." Dorothy knelt down and put her floppy hat on the ground. Four yellow chicks scurried out chirping and trotting around in the dusty grass.

"Oh great!" said Barbara. "We can have roast chicken."

"Well hopefully we'll get some eggs and offspring from them before they go in the pot," joked Dorothy.

The embers in the fire were still glowing from their morning tea. Dorothy brought it alive and put the kettle on the fire. By late afternoon the girls' fridge was finished. It stood about two feet off the ground on wooden legs. The box-shaped structure on the legs measured about 2 feet square and consisted of a double layer of gauze on all four sides and on the top and bottom of the box. They had packed pieces of charcoal between the layers of gauze leaving no gaps. There had been mounds of burnt wood near a rubbish dump and they had picked out the best pieces. The door was bound several times on one side with baling wire and it served, only just, as a hinge.

The girls had instructed Dorothy not to look at their work of art until it was finished. She promised not to and had a good excuse sit under the acacia tree with her back to the activity and shut her eyes.

She had almost dozed off when Diana asked her to stand up. Dorothy obliged and Diana put her hands over Dorothy's eyes feeling Diana's little hand over her right eye.

"OK, you can look!" said Diana excitedly and took her hands away.

"Well I never. A thing of beauty is a joy forever!" laughed Dorothy. "Goodness, is *that* a fridge?"

"Yes," said all three girls together.

"And it works," said Betty.

"Well we don't have anything to put in it yet," said Diana.

"Yes we do." Dorothy went into her hut and brought out a plastic bag. "I did a bit of shopping this morning. Here, let's put these soup bones and a loaf of bread in our new fridge. We'll see in a few hours if they're still cool!"

They had survived another day in their strange existence. They had finished supper and washed the dishes. A regular routine was falling into place. They sat by the fire as it hissed and crackled and Barbara threw a log on the dwindling flames. The African sky was particularly dark and enhanced the star-studded canopy above. Chirping crickets in the nearby bush gave an air of mystery to the night and the croaking frogs signalled the end of spring and the heralding of the first rains of summer.

The soup bones had survived very well in their newfound fridge. They were an economical buy as they had a meal each day from them for a week. Their one meal a day was supper and each night it was the same. The stewed soup bones made gravy, which they had with cabbage and posho. Dorothy was managing to stretch out the money they had. They prepared a vegetable garden with Esther's blessings. The farm had an excellent underground water supply and was pumped into corrugated iron tanks by strategically placed windmills. Dorothy had had the foresight to bring their hosepipe from the house and Esther had allowed them to use as much water as they wanted for their veggie garden. The girls brought bucket loads of kraal manure from the cattle pens and forked it into the watered beds. They were ready for seeds.

It was a week since Dorothy had seen Charles. They were out of soup bones and Dorothy was keen to get some seeds for their new beds. She decided to kill two birds with one stone, visit Charles and do her necessary shopping.

They had been living in the huts for almost four months. Charles would be out of prison in six weeks. Dorothy's money had run out. She had been conservative with it and it lasted surprisingly well she thought. Their vegetables were growing well, the summer rains far more beneficial than their hand watering. They had tomatoes, beans, onions, cabbage and potatoes. The chickens were producing eggs and they now had six additional chickens.

The girls had made friends with the labourers' children on the farm and improved their Swahili so they were almost fluent, although their Nairobi gardener Sixpence had taught them a lot of the local language. They also introduced them to posho, made like a stiff porridge from crushed maize. They'd eat it with their fingers and learnt to make it into a small ball then push their thumb into the middle to make an indentation to scoop up gravy. They'd nibble around the edges of the ball careful not to breach the gravy hole.

The girls would swap the vegetables with mangos, guavas and gooseberries, which the other children got from a nearby farm. They loved eating mangos that were messy and sticky but juicy and sweet.

The hairy pips were put to good use and when lathered with soap, were useful for washing.

It hadn't rained for a few weeks but the rains were like that in Africa. There would be a deluge then nothing for weeks on end. Dorothy had attached their hosepipe to the nearby standpipe and was busy watering the vegetable garden when she saw Esther appear from the direction of her house. She seldom paid a visit.

"Hello Esther."

"Hello," said Esther. "Your husband must be due for release soon." She was to the point as usual.

"Yes. He'll be out in a month." Dorothy wondered if her question was leading anywhere.

"What do you propose doing when he's out?"

"Well," Dorothy hesitated and was beginning to feel uneasy. "We're not sure. We're hoping he'll be able to find another job."

"You're welcome to stay here until you find somewhere else. You're vegetable garden's doing well."

"Thank you," Dorothy was relieved. "I'll send the girls over later with some pickings. Anything in particular you'd like?" They often took vegetables to Esther, which she appreciated.

"No, anything you send over is put to good use. Thank you. I wanted to tell you Girlie left about a month ago. She said she'd found a job in town." The plump woman left without saying anything further.

Dorothy was devastated. She hadn't seen her for a while but wasn't overly concerned. Why, she wondered, did she go without saying goodbye? After all those years of being together? Perhaps she just didn't want to say goodbye.

Diana had become chief cook and enjoyed preparing the meals. They hadn't had any meat for some months other than soup bones.

"Mummy, can we eat a chicken?" Diana was preparing the evening meal.

"Oh dear. I was wondering when one of you would suggest that. Do you *really* want to do that?"

"Yes of course. A few of them aren't laying now anyway. Can we? Please?" pleaded Diana.

"Let's think about it tomorrow."

Tomorrow arrived too soon for Dorothy. Diana may have had a deformed hand but there was nothing wrong with her mind or memory.

"Can we have a chicken for supper tonight?" asked Diana. "Betty said she'd kill it for us."

"Oh alright. I'm sure it'll be very nice," said Dorothy.

"Woopie." Diana ran into Betty and Barbara's hut and told them the good news.

The sun was high and execution time was nigh and duties had been allocated. Barbara was the youngest and fastest and would catch the doomed chicken. Betty was the oldest and meanest and would perform the execution. Diana would remain in the galley and Dorothy? She'd be referee on the sidelines.

The clucking started and Barbara headed towards the doomed lady. The clucking intensified. Barbara held out her arms and her bony tanned legs moved faster and faster. She neared the marked feathered woman and the clucking changed to shrieks. Wings flapped, feathers and grass flew and Barbara rugby-dived the fleeing bird. She got it. Its wings beat her on the face and head and she tucked the condemned bird under her arm, curtailing its onslaught.

"Your turn," said Barbara and handed the bird to Betty.

"Hmm," said Betty. "The moment of truth. Not sure if I want to do this." She had a large kitchen knife in her hand and walked up to a big granite rock not far from the fire. "The quickness of the hand deceives the eye," and she sliced off the chickens head on the rock. Betty screamed and dropped the knife and the chicken and ran towards Diana and Barbara. "Oh, that was terrible," said Betty, squirming.

"Look, look," screamed Barbara. The headless chicken was running around in circles, blood dripping from the hole in the top of its neck.

"Just look away girls. It's just muscular reflexes. It will stop in a minute." Dorothy was right as it collapsed in no time.

"Who's going to skin it?" asked Diana.

"Not me," said Barbara. "You can do it Betty. You're the biggest and ugliest."

"Why do I have to do all the dirty work? I want the biggest helping then. We'd better boil some water."

"You don't skin a chicken darling, you de-feather it," Dorothy corrected Diana.

They hadn't had anything so tasty for several months and they ate in silence, savouring every mouthful.

"That was absolutely delicious," said Dorothy as she nibbled and sucked a drumstick. "You're a good little cook my darling. Thank you."

"Yeah, thanks. Really tasty," concurred Betty.

"Hmmm," came Barbara's approval as she licked every last drop on her plate.

"We should have had this for Daddy's homecoming," said Dorothy.

Diana giggled. "We'll have another one!"

Charles' release day arrived and they'd arranged between them on Dorothy's last visit weeks earlier, that she'd collect him. She left the girls early in the morning and started her long trek to the prison. She had no alternative now but to walk, her small amount of savings exhausted. A few cars passed her on the main road but they didn't stop. She arrived at the prison at 10.30, later than she had anticipated. The wooden doors were closed and there was no one in sight. She knocked on the door using the metal knocker. She thought no one would hear but she heard footsteps on the other side of the door. The wooden slat slid back on the peephole in the door.

"Yes?" came a voice from the face in the peephole.

"I've come to see my husband Charles Butler. He's due for release today."

The slat slammed shut and she heard the bolts sliding on the smaller door. It opened and a warder beckoned her in.

"Thank you," said Dorothy.

"Come with me," said the warder. The warder took her to an office off the courtyard. "Wait here," he said.

She waited, and waited and waited. It was 11.30 and she wondered if the warder had forgotten her. Another fifteen minutes passed when she heard footsteps, then keys unlocking the door to the office. It opened and Charles came sheepishly through the door. His hair had grown into a short crew cut. He was wearing a dark blue suit, white shirt and his army regimental tie. His clothes hung on him, his eyes were sunken and lifeless and Dorothy responded to his nervous smile They hugged each other.

"Come on," barked the warder. He led them to the little wooden door at the entrance and opened it. "Off you go."

They both said "thank you" simultaneously.

They walked in silence for a few minutes. "It's good to be out," said Charles. "Where are we going?"

"To the farm and the huts. The girls are waiting to see you. We'll have to walk."

"That's alright," said Charles. He took off his jacket and slung it over his shoulder.

It was mid afternoon by the time they arrived at the huts. The girls saw them on the dust road and ran to greet them.

"Daddy we've missed you." Betty hugged Charles for a long time with Diana and Barbara queuing nearby.

"My darlings, my darlings. I'm so, so sorry." There were tears in his eyes.

"Come." Diana didn't want to see him crying. "We've got the kettle on."

It was dusk and they all sat around the fire. The girls had been busy during the day and another non-productive chicken had been decapitated and the smell of it cooking in the pot had their juices running. They were having pot roasted potatoes, beans and gravy with their beautifully basted chicken.

"It's unbelievable what you've done. The veggie garden, the chickens and of course the home made fridge. I'm so proud of you all. The huts are cosy and homely. You've done wonders my darling." Charles held Dorothy's hand and kissed her on the cheek. No one mentioned why they were there and the cause of the total upheaval in their lives. It was too sensitive to even think about right now.

The sleeping arrangements were reorganised. Dorothy and Charles were to have one hut and the three girls shared the other. In their innovative fashion, they had made a camp bed of sorts for Diana. They had cut the rubber tube of an old car tyre into thick strips and nailed them to a low, wooden framed bed. The hammock type strips were padded with layer upon layer of thatching grass they had gathered in the bush and that was covered with a blanket. A tight squeeze but it fitted into Betty and Barbara's hut.

Charles lay with his arm around Dorothy. He had dreamt of this moment for months. They had a lot to talk about but they lay quietly, silently respecting each other's thoughts. He was up before dawn accustomed to prison routine. He slipped out of bed so not to disturb Dorothy. He had never set a fire in his life but Diana had the necessary dry grass and chips of wood neatly stacked with the large logs. Flames were leaping into the air in no time, he added logs to the fire and placed the blackened tatty enamel kettle over the flames. He'd make everyone a cup of tea and also use the hot water to shave.

He sat on a granite stone near the fire. The wild birds were getting noisier as the eastern sky lightened. The smell of the bush, the grass and the odd whiff of smoke were pleasing to Charles. He poured boiling water into his enamel shaving-mug and left the kettle balancing on a rock next to the fire. Too early for tea he thought. The put his mirror on the large granite rock and propped it up with a log of wood. The cooing doves signalled the sunrise, the yellow eastern sky brightening and mingling with a silver glow. The Starlings started their chorus. The bush was coming alive.

He was still shaving when Dorothy came out of the hut in her usual khaki shorts, cotton shirt and sandals. She poked the fire and put the kettle on the wire gauze. The trees were making long eerie shadows across the bush now as the sun glided above the treetops. Charles used the towel over his shoulder to wipe the excess soap from his face and greeted Dorothy.

"Hello darling."

"Hi," she replied sleepily. "What's on the agenda for today?"

"Well, I thought I'd go to town and look for a job. There're a few engineering firms around."

"Yes, alright. What's happened to that civil case? Remember, you were paying half your salary to the clerk of the civil court? What happened about that?"

"Oh heavens, yes," replied Charles. "I don't know why it slipped my mind. I was served with a civil summons a few weeks ago. Blast,

I'd forgotten. It's in my jacket pocket," said Charles and disappeared into the hut. He appeared minutes later with a piece of paper in his hand. "Bloody hell. Next week. I've got to appear in the civil court. Oh hell Dorothy. I'm sick of this."

"Whose fault is that?" Dorothy poked the fire, disinterested. That roller-coaster ride hadn't stopped. "I don't know what to say Charles. This whole thing is a nightmare. You haven't got two pennies to rub together and you still owe money. I just give up."

Charles walked to town every day and came back each day, dejected and empty-handed. He had approached dozens of people and companies. It seemed to be a case of not what you know but who you know. He couldn't mention Harvey. They'd want to know why he left there. He was in a no win situation. Charles didn't approach Sir Edmund. That would have been a waste of time seeing he couldn't or wasn't able to help Dorothy.

Dorothy accompanied him to court for the civil hearing. He still owed around £1500 on his first debt. Dorothy was convinced he would be sent to prison again. They were half an hour early for the hearing and they both sat in the back of the courtroom listening to other cases.

Charles' heart sank when the court orderly called his name. He stood in the dock while the prosecutor scratched through the files on his desk. He found the file and read through a document.

"If I may approach the bench, your Worship," said the prosecutor.

"Yes Mr Prosecutor. What is it?" asked the magistrate.

The prosecutor handed a document to the magistrate. He was frowning as he read it. "Right thank you." The magistrate looked at Charles. "Are you Charles Butler?"

"Yes sir."

"The plaintiff in this case, Roger McMinn, has withdrawn the civil suit against you. This court duly withdraws the case. You are free to go."

Charles thought he was hearing things. "Do you mean I don't owe Mr McMinn anything now?"

"That's correct Mr Butler."

Charles continued to stand in the dock. He didn't know what to do.

"You can go now," said the court orderly.

Dorothy accompanied him out of the courtroom. "The devil looks after his own so they say. It's unbelievable." She wasn't excited, just relieved.

"Unbelievable isn't the word. It's a miracle," said Charles. "What worries me is the £3000 I borrowed from Ted Jones, you know, the fraud case. I'm wondering if he's going to make a civil claim for that."

"You're a pain Charles, a real pain in the posterior." Dorothy was so fed up with him.

"I don't want it hanging over my head. Tell you what; Ted's office is not far from here. I want to see him."

"What will that achieve? You can't pay him anyway."

"I just want to see what he intends doing, that's all. Come, let's go."

Dorothy waited outside the building and Charles went inside to see Ted. He knew where his office was and climbed the stairs to the first floor and walked half way along a passage. He hoped he was there. He knocked and heard Ted telling him to come in. Good, he thought.

"Hello Ted," said Charles.

"Huh, well I'm damned. I thought they'd locked you up," said Ted.

"I served six months."

"You should've served six bloody years, you bastard."

"I'm sorry Ted, I'm really sorry. I've lost my job and I don't know when I can re-pay you." Charles was genuinely concerned.

"I know damn well I'll never see my money. It's history, a bad debt. I'm glad you rotted in prison but it should've been longer. You're a fucking thief. Get out of my office. I don't want to see your bloody face again." Ted was red in the face. He opened the door, "Out, get out."

"I'm sorry Ted. Thank you." Charles made a hasty exit.

Charles joined Dorothy downstairs. "This is my lucky day. He doesn't want to see me again."

"What do you mean?"

"He's laughed it off as a bad debt," said Charles.

"So you don't owe anything and you don't have any money. Hey-ho, we're back to square one I suppose." Dorothy was far from excited.

"Well at least the slate's wiped clean."

"Yes, wiped clean with a dirty cloth. It still leaves a mark Charles. Let's go home, if we can call it home."

Weeks passed and Charles walked to town each day job hunting but came home empty handed. The girls continued to amuse themselves and had made a swing, tied in the branches of their acacia tree. They'd leap off the granite rock, swing high in the air and the rope would twist and shorten then unravel in a dizzy spin.

Dorothy would attend to the vegetable garden and do mundane chores like washing and ironing. She had a huge heavy iron with a hinged lid and was designed to take red-hot coals. It worked perfectly and the ironing was done on the carpeted floor in her hut. The routine frustrated Dorothy knowing their lives couldn't go on like that forever. She thought more and more about the only option that would get them out of the squalid lifestyle they were living. Would it change their lives for the better she kept asking herself over and over again. She knew she had to do it.

They were all at their lowest ebb and they retired to their huts early one evening, earlier than usual as Dorothy wanted to tell Charles her plan.

"You do know we can't carry on living like this." She started the conversation. "I think we should all go to England. You're not going to find work here."

"All well and good but we can't pay for a bus fare Dorothy, let alone travel to England."

Dorothy was quiet for a while. She had kept this a secret all through their marriage and hadn't told anyone but she had no choice now. "I have a piece of jewellery given to me by my late husband, the Belgium Baron. I had it valued in Hong Kong years ago and it will get us to England with some change."

"Huh, and you let me go to prison?" snorted Charles.

"Don't speak like that. I'm not going to spend my entire life bailing you out of your bloody debts. I have the girls to think about. You are bloody selfish Charles, bloody, bloody selfish." Dorothy was shouting at him and had lost her temper completely. She was in no mood to be anywhere near him. "Damn you, you make me sick." She stormed out of the hut slamming the rickety door behind her but it made insufficient noise to vent her anger. She put all her force behind it again and slammed it so hard against the frame that it flew back and hung on one hinge. The girls had heard every word and they wondered where all this would lead.

Dorothy spent the night in a deck chair outside. The night was humid but she stoked the fire, the flames and sparks her only companion for the night. Although tired, she only dozed off after midnight and was woken by the sound of Charles putting the kettle on the fire.

She wasted no time and left for town with the necklace she hoped would change their lives. As she recalled, the jeweller in Hong Kong had valued it at £4000. She was sure it had been under valued as the four diamonds were very big. She went straight to a jewellery shop and a little man came to the counter from the back of the shop.

"Good morning. I want to sell this necklace. Would you be interested and what would you give me for it." Dorothy took the necklace out of a black drawstring bag and handed it to the man. He swung the magnifying glass over his eye from a gadget on his head and studied the necklace.

"Hmm, impressive. I'll need to weigh the diamonds. Could you hold on a moment?" The little man went behind a glass partition and she saw him fiddling with her prize possession. He returned and said, "This is a fine piece of jewellery madam. I can offer you £5,000 for it."

Dorothy didn't hesitate and accepted the man's offer. He was surprised at her request for cash but obliged after drawing cash from his bank. She wanted to jump for joy. She needed to think for a moment and went to a tearoom above a departmental store.

She realised what a rough life they were living as she drank her tea out of a fine china teacup again, with starched linen on the table. They had nothing to keep them in Kenya now. She was going to book their trip back to England.

She went straight to a travel agency in Nairobi. A mail ship was leaving Mombassa for England in ten days. The next one was in two months. She made the booking including their train journey to the coast. It was done, decision made. They were leaving for England in ten days. She had a lot of change, which gave her a sense of security. Dorothy walked back to the huts. She had enough change for a few trips to England but she'd learnt what it was like to be without any money and taught her to be conservative with finances.

The ten days flew by. They said their farewells to Esther and left all the bits and pieces they weren't able to take, including their well established vegetable garden. The farm labourers had become good friends and the girls had played many games with their children and the girls were going to miss their new friends.

The ship sailed early afternoon. The girls nattered continuously which made up for Dorothy's and Charles' silence. They stayed on deck for hours leaning on the portside rails as the ship ploughed through the Indian Ocean, north along the African coast that would take them past Aden, through the Red Sea and the narrow Suez Canal and they couldn't help but reminisce.

Diana recalled the years in their big house in Nairobi and Girlie. Girlie used to tease them with stories about the Masai, the fierce tribe that drifted across Kenya with their cattle. They were *told* they were fierce but they later learnt from the children on the farm that they were quite harmless and liked to keep to themselves leading a nomadic life. Girlie had given the impression they were terrifying bogeymen. When the girls were naughty Girlie would threaten to call the Masai and have them taken away in sacks. Diana was terrified some nights, lying in her bed in the dark, thinking an old Masai man was under her bed. The fear was so real to her she'd take a huge leap off her bed, so he wouldn't catch her legs and Diana recalled how she made a mad dash down the passage to Dorothy's room. Dorothy was a poor sleeper and no matter when Diana sped to her, she would be awake, reading. She would hear Diana coming and had her bedclothes turned back ready for her to leap in beside her.

Barbara remembered the short holiday they took to Jinja on the shores of Lake Victoria in Uganda. Their bedroom was a hut and she recalled how they lay awake listening to something grunting and scraping the walls of their round hut. They had thought it was elephants and she remembered how Dorothy had told them it was hippos coming up from the lake at night and scraping the mud off their huge bodies.

The coast was almost on the horizon now and the African sun was setting, a huge red ball balancing majestically in the dusty haze above a silent, enchanting continent. Yes, they were going to miss Africa.

CHAPTER 6

L ondon 1930. Dorothy knew London well and she found them
a comfortable hotel. The girls were used to the freedom of
running wild in Africa and were frustrated being confined to a
hotel room. They were not permitted in the lounges and dining room
and had their meals in the children's dining room.

Their boredom led them to a new game, devised by Betty. They
got the pillows off their beds and slung them over the banister.
They'd climbed on, then slide down swiftly to the hotel foyer with
screams of delight and to the astonishment of the manager and
guests. The game was short-lived, as was their stay at the respectable
hotel. They were called little monsters by the hotel staff.

They moved to another hotel and Dorothy employed a governess
for the girls for a few months. Her name was Olive and she took the
girls on frequent walks in the parks and squares. The girls didn't
particularly like Olive and led her on a merry dance. They gave her
the slip in a square one day and dragged a few park benches together
and made a 'den'.

An irate park keeper approached them. "Eh, what ya think ya
doin'?" he shouted.

The girls looked at him blankly, turned to each other and broke into Swahili and said,

"Shenzi sana kabesa."* * Roughly translated as 'nasty piece of work.'

"You little savages," was the keeper's response.

The girls laughed and ran off, leaving the man to straighten the benches. They continued to play in the square and enjoyed climbing the trees, reminding them of their carefree days in Africa. They returned to the hotel dirty but happy.

Charles was away a lot and had a job with the railways. Dorothy was able to give them a bit of pocket money and they handled money for the first time in their lives. They would buy marshmallow fish and liquorice strips, always their favourites. As the year progressed they moved from hotels to boarding houses and the girls were aware that their financial position was changing dramatically and there seemed to be no money for anything. Dorothy was keeping the upper hand with Charles and was receiving his pay each month. She had to rely on his fervent promises to her that he wouldn't borrow or get into debt. He drifted in and out of work, doing contract work here and there. His salary kept a roof over their heads.

Winter arrived and the girls had few toys with them, only the ones they had brought with them from Kenya. They had snakes and ladders, ludo, tiddlywinks and cards that kept them occupied and out of mischief. They did go for walks and were fascinated by a well-muffled figure cooking chestnuts on top of a charcoal brazier. The girls were allowed to buy a few and warmed their gloved hands around them. It was a far cry from Africa.

Dorothy woke the girls one night in the boarding house. She was excited and took them onto the balcony of her room. "Look," she said and pointed into the sky.

They saw a beautiful silver cigar-shaped object sailing silently overhead.

"Look at it carefully, it's an airship. You might never see one like it again." They watched as it slowly went out of sight.

Dorothy had some sad new for them the next day. "Remember the airship last night. It was called the R101 and it was on its maiden voyage. It crashed in France today and killed everyone onboard."

"What's a maiden voyage?" asked Barbara.

"It means it was it's first voyage."

Dorothy recalled her decision not to go on the Titanic's maiden voyage and wondered if she made the wrong choice.

Christmas was very quiet but they were together. Charles had work but spent the holidays with the family. A box of Plasticine kept them occupied for hours. They wasted no time and started making African villages with little huts; minute native figures in colourful 'clothes,' round three legged cooking pots, pestle and mortars, a woman complete with child on her back crushing maize for the posho. It was quite an achievement and depicted a typical African village. It sent a heart-felt message to Dorothy and Charles that they longed for Africa and wanted to go home.

Things didn't improve in 1932. Dorothy was clearly not happy in London and neither were the girls.

"Mummy, can't we go back to Africa?" asked Barbara one day.

"I think we all want to go back darling. Daddy is getting work, sometimes part time work, but he isn't happy here either."

"Is he in debt again?" quizzed Betty openly. They knew all about the problems before.

"No, he's not," said Dorothy. "He gives me his pay each month and he promised me faithfully he'd behave himself."

"Have we got enough money to go back?" asked Diana.

"We'll have to see," replied Dorothy. She didn't want to go into detail with them.

Dorothy knew they had to return to Africa -s omehow.

Charles returned home in February, having completed a two-month contract. He was concerned that the family were not happy in England. "How do you feel about returning to Africa darling?"

"You know we all want to go back," said Dorothy. "Africa's a big place. Where are we going to go?"

"I've been thinking about South Africa, possibly Cape Town as a steppingstone. There's a lot of work there and in the Colonies. There'll be lots of advertisements for jobs in the major newspapers."

"We've managed to save a bit which has been a miracle but it won't get us to Cape Town", said Dorothy. They had never discussed the sale of her necklace in Nairobi. Charles had been all too aware of his antics and was embarrassed, even ashamed to ask Dorothy what she sold it for. Dorothy on the other hand, although she liked to be straight with Charles, never told him in fear he'd go off the rails again. She was concerned, above all else, for the welfare of the girls. It was an unwritten law between them. "I'll make enquiries tomorrow and find out what it would cost."

They talked for hours into the night. The girls heard the discussions behind their bedroom door. They had no idea what it was about but felt sure it had to be something exciting.

Charles took the girls for a walk the next day and Dorothy headed off on her own, well able to handle the family affairs. She went from travel agent to travel agent all offering different prices on passenger liners travelling to all the continents. They all varied but she found one that excited her. She could easily manage the fares and she returned to the boarding house with a bounce in her step.

Charles returned with the girls after dark. Dorothy was excited but tried to contain herself until she had agreed with Charles and made the final decision to go. They ate supper earlier than usual and the girls were herded off to play in their room.

Charles had noticed something different about Dorothy, an aura he couldn't explain but he knew it was something good. "Did you make any headway today?" he asked.

"Yes, I think I found a good bargain." She was keen to tell him. "There's a passenger-carrying cargo ship leaving Tilbury next week for Cape Town. The agent agreed to hold five bookings until tomorrow. He said there weren't many left."

"That sounds wonderful!" Charles seldom found moments of excitement. "Now," he was more controlled, "The million dollar question. Can we afford it?"

"We'll use your savings and I'll be able to scrape the balance together," Dorothy lied. She didn't feel guilty either. She just wasn't telling him the size of her nest egg. It was to remain in the family 'vault' and only she had the key.

They all went with Dorothy to the travel agent. The girls were ecstatic and were dancing and jumping all over the pavement, speaking fluent Swahili to each other much to the horror of local pedestrians. Dorothy treated them to tea and cakes at a very nice tearoom. They were so excited Dorothy and Charles could hardly contain them.

"Stop it now," said Dorothy. "Try and behave like ladies, if that's possible. We're only going to Africa!" Dorothy was as excited as they were.

They set sail a week later, along the English Channel, through the Bay of Biscay and into the Atlantic.

CHAPTER 7

The ship anchored briefly off Tenerife in the Canary Islands where they experienced the narrow winding cobbled streets, the tiers of white buildings and masses of people in their flowing colourful robes. Their marrow warmed to the suns rays extending beyond the delectably near tropic of cancer.

As they sailed further south the weather changed and it became colder, the sea rougher and the little cargo ship pitched and rolled in the South Atlantic Ocean, the girls thinking the journey would never end. They were still sleeping early one morning in their box-like cabin when Dorothy came in.

Come," she said excitedly. "I've got something to show you."

The girls clambered up the narrow metal steps onto the deck.

"Look over there, land, and there's Table Mountain!"

They had arrived at the tip of Africa, a long way from the equator and the tropical heat they knew so much but nevertheless it was Africa.

They stayed in a modest hotel in Cape Town. Charles was out each day scouring the newspapers for work either in South Africa or the Colonies in the North.

"I thought I'd have found something by now."

"We've only been here a week Charles. I'm sure something will materialise." Dorothy had to be positive.

She was right. Charles read through the vacancies columns of three papers the next day and something caught his eye.

"Here we are. The Shire Highlands Railways are looking for surveyors. Contract work in *Nyasaland!* How about that?"

"The girls would probably like it. Yes, why not? Where do you write?"

"Let me see. Oh, Johannesburg. They must have a head office there, that's useful."

Charles read the small print at the end of the advertisement. "Interviews in Johannesburg *and* Cape Town. That's great. Shall we go for it?"

"*You* go for it! Start writing and get it posted chop-chop." Dorothy had spoken.

It all happened at lightning speed. Charles attended the interview in Cape Town ten days later and was accepted for the post. The family were on the move again. Dorothy was relieved when Charles told her the company would be paying for the re-location. She was keen to hang on to that nest egg for dire emergencies and she had learnt those came around with immense regularity.

The journey took them through the majestic rugged mountains around Paarl in the Cape, the steam train chugging effortlessly in and out of the shadows of the mountains. There was a sense of serenity about it and Dorothy enjoyed the dining car with the silver service, the white starched linen and fine wines, no doubt from the famous vineyards in the area. This was the life she knew. She recalled the high life in London in her early twenties, her marriage to the Belgium Baron and subsequent life in Paris; her journey on the Trans Siberian Railway all those years ago.

"Cheers darling. Here's to happy days." Charles raised his wine glass.

"Happy days," said Dorothy, their glasses clicking. "This is magical. I could live like this forever."

"I hope I can do that for you. I've caused you a lot of heart-ache over the years and it's hurt me as much, I can assure you."

"You've kept your nose clean for a year Charles. It proves you *can* do it. Keep it up my darling."

The family were allocated two compartments in the first class section. The girls had a four-bunk compartment and there were arguments over the two top bunks. Betty and Diana were the oldest and won the argument. Dorothy and Charles had a coupe right next door.

The steam train went through the highveld, the wide-open plains of Southern Africa. They would stop at dusty sidings and watch the Africans holding up their wares at the windows and bartering with passengers. It was nearly winter in Southern Africa. The nights were cold but day after day the skies were cloudless and blue, the sun warm. They travelled northeast into Portuguese Territory and to their final destination on that train journey, the town of Chinde in Tete province. Chinde was a small town on the southern shores of the mighty Zambezi River that flowed into the Indian Ocean and they had to cross the great river to reach Nyasaland situated north of the river.

There was no station at Chinde and they disembarked onto red earth and the girls ran along the side of the train to see the huge Garrett engine still hissing and puffing at the head of the train. There were plenty of willing African porters who took their luggage to the paddle steamer tied up at the nearby jetty on the river.

"You didn't tell us we're going on this?" Betty was excited.

"You don't know *everything*, although you all think you do sometimes," joked Dorothy. "Nyasaland is up country on the other side of the river. They're taking us up the river in the steamer to a place called Tete and then on *another* train to Limbe."

"Everyone aboard," shouted a man with a white cap. The engines were turning over gently and smoke drifted slowly from the chimneystack. The passengers sat on benches on the low deck, luggage piled in a confined area. African men were strategically positioned on either side of the steamer with their long bamboo poles at the ready in the event of hitting sand banks.

The ropes were thrown aboard and as the gurgling diesel engines burst into a purring crescendo the wooden paddle wheel at the rear of the steamer came to life. The paddle churned the muddy river water and they moved away slowly from the jetty, the start of their long journey up the Zambezi to Tete on the northern shores.

The steamer ran into sand banks many times on the trip, the Africans pushing it free with their bamboo poles as they sang lustily, a throbbing chant keeping in time with the thrusting poles. They were an impressive sight, naked to the waist, their strong muscled backs bending to the task. They saw groups of hippo, their dome-shaped heads and massive snouts jutting out of the water like silent statues, only the involuntary flicking of their ears bringing them to life. The girls were over the moon. This was the life they loved.

They reached Tete at dusk with plenty of bustling and shouting all around, the train waiting to take passengers to Limbe. Charles pointed out the engraved name on the train windows. "See that. 'Shire Highlands Railways!' That's interesting."

The train arrived in Limbe late into the night. There was a yawning sense of deliverance, the real smells and sounds of Africa. Everyone making a din, voices jabbering in the darkness with lanterns bobbing about nearby and in the shadowy bush. They all felt so at home. Someone was there to meet them and they drove to their rented house.

The next six months flew by. They were well settled in their large rambling old house, with veranda's all around and gauze to keep the insects out. There was no electricity but paraffin lamps were everywhere. It was luxury compared to their huts in Nairobi. The garden was huge with vegetable gardens and an array of trees for the girls to climb.

The girls attended a convent school run by nuns from different nationalities. Their education had been sadly neglected and they had difficulty catching up. Charles was very busy with his engineering and survey work, which was done locally enabling him to be with the family until a temporary transfer came up.

"Dorothy, I've got to move to Blantyre for about six months. The company has a contact up there. I'll be staying in a small cottage on Mr Ramsey's property."

"Oh, Mr Ramsey no less! *The* big boss! I'm sure not may employees can boast about that. When are you going?"

"In about ten days but that has to be confirmed. I'll be driving up with my equipment. Will you be alright on your own with the girls?"

"That's a silly question Charles. My concern is you. Things have been fine since we left Kenya and I don't want you going off the rails again."

"For heavens sake Dorothy. I'll be fine."

"Charles, I'm going with you."

"This is a short company contract and the family is not expected to tag along. In any event, the cottage is probably very small and not suitable for you. I doubt Mr Ramsey would be expecting you."

"I don't care. I'm *not* going to sit here for six months, wondering what you are up to. Forget it Charles. I'm coming and that's that. The cottage can't be worse than those huts in Kenya."

"Please Dorothy. Be reasonable. Anyway, what about the girls?"

"There are boarding facilities at the convent and the girls can board for the six months.

We just cannot afford to have our lives ruined again with your gambling. You'll be on your own up there, you'll get bored at night and before you know it you'll be with the boys. Either I come with you or I'm going back to South Africa with the girls."

Dorothy arranged with the Mother Superior at the convent that the girls board for six months. They were excited at the prospect but concerned their freedom would be curtailed but they knew it couldn't be worse than the boarding houses in London.

"Come on girls. Jump in." Dorothy was taking them to school that day, with their suitcases of clothing ready to start their six months of boarding.

"This is like going to prison for six months," said Barbara.

"Yes, we're following in father's footsteps," joked Diana.

"Enough of that," snapped Dorothy as she drove her three hooligans down the driveway. All three sat in the back seat to avoid the arguments as to who would sit in the front. They wore their uniforms and big floppy hats, their luggage piled high in the front seat and the boot.

Dorothy saw them settled in to the one and only dormitory with a few other girls. She hugged them individually and promised to collect them for the school holidays. She drove away from the convent feeling empty. They had never been separated before and she smiled nervously when she wondered how they would behave. It would be good clean fun she thought and no doubt the nuns would keep them under control.

Dorothy and Charles spent their last night in the house in Limbe. It was like a morgue without the girls. Charles loaded the pickup in the morning with his survey equipment.

Their journey to Blantyre was on narrow dust roads with changing scenery. They drove through miles of fertile land, grassy plains as far as the eye could see, dotted with small African settlements depicted by groups of grass huts. They went through forests and past rushing streams. Local Africans walked along the road, some carrying wood or buckets of maize on their heads whilst others herding goats and cattle. The wide-open spaces gave a sense of peace and freedom. Dorothy often felt torn between the culture and fine life she had been accustomed to and to this vast, serene, wild continent, her senses kept drawing her to the latter.

They arrived in Blantyre late in the afternoon. They stopped outside a shop in the dusty streets of the town and asked the Indian storekeeper for directions to Mr Ramsey's house. It was said everyone knew where the 'railway boss' lived. Sure enough, the little round Indian man gave them detailed directions in his broken English, to the 'very very big house' on the 'mountain.' Their pick-up struggled up a steep driveway and they saw the massive house looming out of the dusk. It was a beautiful Dutch gabled design with huge double wooden doors and natural wood shutters on the windows. The lawn went right up to the house with flowerbeds and shrubs of various shapes and sizes dotted over the extensive lawns.

"This is bliss," said Dorothy. "Shall we park in the tradesmen's entrance?" she chuckled. She used the knocker on the wooden doors. "Does this remind you of something?" teased Dorothy.

Charles nudged her on her arm with his elbow. "Don't rub it in."

A tall thin African dressed in a white starched uniform answered the door and they asked for Mr Ramsey. He beckoned them in and told them to wait in the hallway. The walls were packed with mounted animal heads, no doubt trophies from safari hunts. Two huge lion skins lay on the terracotta floor. They must have been magnificent animals, their heads mounted with mouths in a snarling position, eyes fierce amber and protruding red tongues. Dorothy was mesmerized by the beasts and didn't hear their host arrive. He was dressed in long khaki shorts, cotton shirt and leather leggings and boots. His long white wavy hair framed a tanned weathered face. The perfect picture of a 'hands on' man.

"Do you like them?" The very English voice brought her back to reality. "Hello, I'm Ramsey. You must be Butler?" He held his hand out to Charles.

"Yes, how do you do Mr Ramsey. This is my wife, Dorothy."

"Pleasure to meet you my dear." Ramsey took her hand and kissed it. "You have a most attractive wife Butler. Now my dear, Phineas will show you to your quarters." He held Dorothy around the waist for a moment then rang a brass ships bell hanging in the hall near the front door.

The man in white who had answered the door for them appeared from nowhere.

"Phineas, will you take this lady to her quarters and help her with her luggage please. There's a good man. Now Butler will you come with me for a moment." Ramsey had clearly taken charge.

They went into an office the size of a huge drawing room. The walls were panelled with wood and two sides were filled with shelf upon shelf of books. There was a draughtsman's table in the corner, illuminated by a dim light on a metal arm. Ramsey explained to Charles his requirements over the coming months.

Charles said goodnight to Ramsey two hours later and found his was to his quarters, a small one-bedroom cottage some two hundred yards from the main house. It was very comfortable with a sitting room, kitchen and bathroom. Gauze frames fitted in each window with a wooden gauzed frame in the doorway. Dorothy had bathed and was cooking in the kitchen.

"Knock knock," said Charles and walked into the kitchen. "This is cosy, isn't it?"

"Yes, I'm impressed. I found some food in the kitchen and meat in the fridge. How do you fancy curry and rice?"

"Mmmm. Sounds great. Old Ramsey seems to fancy you," said Charles casually.

"Do I sense a little jealousy? I'm honoured," she joked. "Charles darling, come off it, he's old enough to be my grandfather."

"Yes, that's the problem. The older they are, the worse they are." They both knew they were engaged in a fun, nonsensical conversation.

"What's that sound of a motor in the distance? It hasn't stopped all evening." Dorothy was stirring the curry on the little two plate stove.

"It's a generator. Runs on diesel. Pretty effective according to Ramsey and provides electricity to the main house, this cottage and the staff quarters. You probably had a hot bath. He says it heats the geysers."

"Luxurious camping. Glad I came with you! Keep your nose clean Charles and make my life easy." She gave him a quick kiss and got back to the stove.

They enjoyed their meal on a tiny but adequate table in the sitting room. The lights flickered intermittently in unison with the generator as it coughed and spluttered in the darkness way beyond the staff quarters.

Charles had to be up before dawn and they were in bed early. It was a small double bed on a terracotta floor with loose colourful Indian carpets scattered on the floor. An old wooden wardrobe stood in the corner with hanging space and draws, quite adequate for their six-month stay. Dorothy slid under the white starched sheets next to Charles and lay back on the pillows, tired but content. Charles rolled over and lay next to her and tried to kiss her.

"Charles darling. I'm not in the mood. I keep thinking about the girls in boarding school and I feel very guilty."

"They'll be fine and they'll love it. I'm sure they're glad to see the back of us for a while." Charles tried to convince her.

"Another time," she pecked him on the mouth and rolled away from him. "Night night."

Charles had gone when Dorothy woke. The room was bright and the sun was well up. She made herself a pot of tea and got dressed, her shorts and sleeveless shirt adequate for the day. She wanted to explore the surroundings in daylight. The garden was extensive and there was a huge orchard at the back of the house. She saw two gardeners and greeted them in Swahili that they barely understood but they muddled through quite well in broken English. They showed her the orchard with dozens of different fruits from guavas to oranges, to avocado pears, bananas, peaches and the end of the orchard had a long wire fence covered in granadillas. The rich soils, hot summer sun and copious rainfall were any gardener's dream.

On the 'mountain' as the Indian shopkeeper had called it, or rather on the steep hill scattered over a wide area on either side of the driveway, were dozens of avocado pear trees almost growing wild and laden with fruit. They hadn't noticed them in the dusk the night before. Dorothy stood halfway down the slope and looked out over the trees and she saw a vast expanse of bush shimmering in the heat stretching as far as the eye could see.

The girls were having a rough time at school. They all shared one dormitory and there was no electricity at the school. They carried paraffin lamps with them at night and some were placed at intervals in the passages and hallways. Avocado pear trees lined the avenue leading to the convent and the girls often had a diet of avocado spread on slices of bread for breakfast lunch and supper. They'd sometimes be given Blanc mange for pudding, a varying treat for their taste buds. The girls were hungry most of the time.

On Sundays they went up the hill above the convent in crocodile formation along a footpath to the big cathedral for the service and was attended by the local Roman Catholic community. They always walked in the same order, Betty in front then Diana and Barbara at the rear. One Sunday they stopped at a little niche in a rocky outcrop to look at a small statue of the Virgin Mary.

Diana spent a long time looking at it. "I think I want to be a nun and float along in my habit saying my rosary."

"Me too," said Barbara as they collected wild flowers and placed them at the feet of the statue. They thought it a wonderful vision of life.

"You'll never be nuns," said Betty. "You're far too naughty. The nuns would never let you in. Come on, we'll be late."

They ran off giggling and laughing knowing Betty was quite right.

It was mid-term and their excitement increased. Dorothy would be picking them up for the school holidays. They waited at the entrance of the convent and were expecting Dorothy at 3 o'clock. They were still in their uniforms with floppy hats, luggage piled neatly. A pickup drove towards the convent along the avenue lined with the avocado's they had grown to hate so much.

"Is that her?" Barbara sounded excited.

"It's not her car," said Diana and as the pickup neared, "Yes, it is Mummy!"

The girls ran around the battered pickup like excited puppies and ran alongside the driver's door as Dorothy brought it to a stop. In her hurry to get out she took her foot off the clutch too soon and it lurched forward and stalled.

"Hello my darling." She wrapped her arms around them and hugged them tightly. They looked thin, their bare skinny arms and legs dangling out of baggy uniforms. Their backs felt bony as she hugged them. "Oh my darlings, you've lost weight."

"They've been starving us," said Diana.

"We're sick of avocado's and bread," came Barbara's contribution.

"What do you mean?" Dorothy was concerned.

"That's all we get for breakfast lunch and supper," said Barbara.

"Yes and sometimes a pudding at night," said Betty.

They were all trying to speak at once, telling Dorothy their tales of woe.

"They don't teach properly. The nuns hand us cards with the task for the lesson written on them," said Diana.

"And we're not allowed to ask any questions. If we talk the nuns tell us to keep quiet," said a concerned Barbara.

"They can't speak English, they're either German or French or…."

Dorothy cut Betty short. "That's it." Dorothy was on the war-path. "Load up the truck girls. I'll be back in a minute." Dorothy stormed into the convent. She knew where Mother Superior's office was and marched straight to the door. It was closed and she hammered on the door. No reply. She knocked harder and the door opened.

Mother Superior looked at her with her head tilted to one side. "Yes my dear?" She had a German accent but spoke good English.

Dorothy wasn't going to weaken with the sight of a sweet little nun in front of her.

"Mother Superior," started Dorothy. "I'm getting horrendous reports from my girls about the treatment they've received here. They were not being fed properly. It seems they've been on a diet of avocado pears. How can they learn if they're handed a card with notes on them *and* not be allowed to ask questions?" Dorothy was enraged and was blurting out anything as she remembered it. "*And to top it all, my girls have lost weight. They're skin and bone."*

Mother Superior looked sweetly at Dorothy, hands clasped together under her habit and head still tilted.

"Well?" snapped Dorothy, her blood pressure rising.

"We're doing the very best we can," came her reply.

Dorothy knew she was wasting her time and wouldn't get satisfactory answers. "Well your best is not good enough for me or the girls. They won't be coming back to the convent next term." She left without waiting for an answer.

The girls were squashed in the cab waiting for Dorothy. She squeezed into the driver's seat. "Right. Let's go home. I've spoken to Mother Superior and told her you're not going back to the convent." Dorothy's eardrums nearly burst with screeches of delight.

"Are we coming with you to Blantyre then?" asked Betty.

"No, that won't work. I don't know what I'm going to do. I'll have to think about it."

Dorothy was to be with the girls for three weeks, during their school holidays. It worried her leaving Charles on his own and as much as she wanted to be with the girls, she was keen to get back to him to keep him on the straight and narrow. She knew it was in the best interests of the girls, which eased her feelings of guilt. It would only be for a few more months.

Limbe was a very small town and they had become friendly with a few families, one in particular was Mr and Mrs Peterkin. Mrs Peterkin was a darling, a motherly woman who always made them feel at home and the girls felt they had always known her. Dorothy kept thinking about them and wondered if the girls could stay with them.

They sat down to supper, the third night out of their prison. Dorothy was feeding them well, filling up their skeletal bodies with plenty of vegetables, roasts, roast potatoes and fresh fruit. Avocados were off the menu.

"Now girls. I will have to go back to Daddy in Blantyre for a few months and I'm wondering what to do with you lot."

"We'll stay here and look after the house," said Betty.

"No you won't. How would you like to stay with Mr and Mrs Peterkin?"

"Ooo, yes please!" said Betty.

"Yippy, we like her. It'll be better than that stupid convent," said Barbara.

"Hmm, OK, but we'd rather be with you." Diana had reservations.

"You know I'd like that but it's not feasible at the moment. Let's go and see them tomorrow."

They all piled into the pickup next morning, all happy to sit in the back. They drove for half an hour on dusty potholed roads, the girls loving the sun beating down on them and the smell of cattle dung and dust. They arrived at the Peterkin's farm with a lovely old rambling granite stone farmhouse, large lawns and exotic plants. They knocked on the door and heard footsteps on the bare wooden floorboards.

"Dorothy my dear," a tall plump woman with rosy cheeks and greying hair stood in the doorway. She was wearing an apron around her waist. "Hello Betty, Diana, Barbara." She remembered their names and they were glad she got the order of priority right. "Come in, come in. It's lovely to see you."

She took them into the sitting room filled with leather couches and chairs. The large low windows and French doors overlooked a swimming pool and lush green lawns. Flamboyant trees with their spreading branches provided a shady backdrop at the bottom of the garden.

"Now make yourselves comfortable and I'll put the kettle on."

"We've got a suggestion to put to you when you come back Jenny!" Dorothy knew she'd oblige.

Mrs Peterkin returned ten minutes later with a tray of tea and buttered scones. "Put me out of my misery!" she joked.

"As you know Charles is working around Blantyre and I've been up there with him. He's been there for three months and has another three to go. We had the girls at the convent in Limbe but it wasn't satisfactory. We're wondering if you'd like to look after the girls for the remaining three months?" She took a cup of tea from Jenny.

"My goodness. We'd love to have your three lovely girls. All to ourselves too! Would you like that girls?" Jenny looked at them.

They all replied together, "Yes Mrs Peterkin."

"Just call me Mrs P. It's much easier. When can they come over?" Jenny was keen to have her guests.

"Well, I only arrived a few days ago. Perhaps in a weeks time, if that suits you?" asked Dorothy.

"Yes, lovely, whenever you're ready Dorothy. We're not going anywhere. What about their schooling?"

"I wanted to ask you about that. I believe there's a private tutor in the area. He uses a motorbike. Do you know him?" asked Dorothy.

"Mr Smallie. He taught my boys and he's first class. I can contact him and ask him to come and see you if you like?" The Peterkins had lived in the area for many years and knew everyone.

"That would be lovely. Thanks Jenny." Charles was earning a good salary and they could easily afford a private tutor. "I'll bring the girls over next Friday and I'll return to Blantyre."

Everything had fallen into place for Dorothy and her brood. The girls got on like a house on fire with Mr Smallie and Dorothy was happy with his credentials and the good reports from Jenny. They were way behind in their education and Mr Smallie was to teach the girls Monday to Friday after they had had another week of holidays. Dorothy took the girls to the Peterkin farm as arranged and when she drove away and waved she felt quite happy that they were in good hands. Mrs P was reluctant to take any board and lodging fees but Dorothy insisted.

The girls had the time of their life on the farm and played ball games on the lawns. There was a netball court, which had been used by the Peterkin boys when they were younger and kept them occupied for hours. Mrs P was a superb cook and they were fed three good meals a day, not to mention the homemade bread and cream scones for tea. They helped her in the kitchen in the evenings with the cooking and washing up. It was an easy life style compared to those hard days in Nairobi. Dorothy made the girls promise they'd never tell anyone about those dark days. It was in their past now and to be forgotten.

Mr Peterkin was a kind quiet spoken man. He was never without his felt bush hat with its wide brim and leopard skin band and Mrs P had to remind him to take it off every time he came in the house. The girls joked about his hat and wondered if he went to bed with it on. He was clean-shaven with a leathery face and a woolly head of black hair greying at the temples.

The girls came in to the house after dark one evening and smelt something delicious. They headed for the kitchen and Mrs P was cooking a leg of lamb.

"Smells good," said Diana. "Can I help you with anything?"

"There's a standpipe in the back garden with mint growing near it. Be a good girl and bring me a handful of leaves."

Diana was always keen to help in the kitchen. "What's this for?" she asked.

"Mint sauce. Haven't you heard of it?" queried Mrs P.

"Nope," answered Diana.

"You have mint sauce with roast lamb. Wash the leaves under the tap then cut the leaves very small and put them in this jug of vinegar," explained Mrs P. "And mind your fingers, you don't want to lose any more!"

"Right, now sprinkle a teaspoon of brown sugar over the mint and leave it to permeate into the vinegar. There, you've learnt something new today."

Betty and Barbara set the dining room table and went to join Diana in the kitchen. Mr P come in and he had his hat on as usual. Mrs P was attending to the vegetables on the stove and had her back to him. "Hat!" she bellowed as a matter of routine, much to the amusement of the girls.

They enjoyed a first class supper of roast lamb, lovely crispy roast potatoes, pumpkin and green beans out of the garden. Pudding consisted of layered sliced pears covered with a sponge, fresh cream poured liberally on each helping.

"Thank you Mrs P," said Barbara. "That was a million times better than avocado sandwiches!"

"Who wants to come with me tomorrow to see the tobacco fields and watch the cattle being dipped?" Mr P knew the answer.

They had a breakfast of scrambled eggs, tomatoes and freshly baked bread then jumped in the back of Mr P's pickup. They drove through miles of tobacco fields and stopped outside the barns. He showed them the bundles of tobacco hanging up to dry from long poles. Big fires were being stoked outside the tobacco barns and kept blowing hot air into the barns to cure the leaves. They were fascinated and loved the strong smoky smells.

They drove on to the cattle pens. Fifty or sixty head of cattle had been herded into a large pen made from sturdy gum poles, and a narrow passage also a gum pole structure, led from the pen to the cattle dip. A gate allowed a few cattle at a time into the passage to prevent chaos and stampeding. Farm labourers whistled and prodded the cattle with sticks, controlling them as they bustled along single file to the dip. They jumped in the deep end one after the other holding their heads high and swam five yards to a sloped shallow end allowing the cattle to walk out of the dip and gather in a holding pen on the other side. The pens were dust bowls from continuous use and the smell of dust and trampled cow dung tunnelled into their nostrils. It was exciting and vibrant.

Charles completed his six month contract in Blantyre and they returned to their house in Limbe with the girls joining them.

They spent another year in Limbe and enjoyed a sociable happy time. Charles miraculously stayed away from his gambling and Dorothy always wondered if he had changed his ways or he never had the opportunity to engage in his horrendous activities from the past. The girls private tutor, Mr Smallie continued to teach them at home and their education progressed in leaps and bounds. He was with them Monday to Friday, mornings and afternoons and at the weekends they'd climb trees, play cricket and generally ran amok like wild animals, anything to let off steam and enjoy themselves.

On Saturdays they'd walk with Dorothy down to the local African market to buy vegetables and eggs. To assure customers the eggs were fresh, the vendors would have an enamel bowl of fresh water on a stand and each egg was tested before handing it over. If they sunk to the bottom of the bowl they were fresh; if they floated they were rejected. The African vendors would cook sweet potatoes in old tins filled with charcoal embers and the girls would eat the deliciously hot potatoes covered in ash but soft and tasty inside.

After church on Sundays they would sometimes accompany Charles up Zomba Mountain. They would drive for miles through the forests and the tea and coffee estates, until they reached the stream where trout fish abounded. He taught the girls to 'tickle' the trout to the surface with his rod and flies. They would proudly take their catches home to Dorothy who knew how to clean them and would roll them in oatmeal and fry them for supper.

They enjoyed the close community life in Limbe for two years and they thought it would last forever. As with all contract work it had to come to an end.

It was time to move on again. They all hated the prospect of going to yet another strange place and starting all over again. Once again the suitcases and trunks came out and the packing started not knowing what lay ahead. Charles had decided they should head for Salisbury in Southern Rhodesia. Mr Ramsey had told Charles it was an up and coming British Colony with good prospects of work. Old Ramsey had his finger on the pulse and Charles was relying on his word.

They boarded the train in Limbe to take them back to Tete on the river and the paddle streamer with the chanting pole-pushers. Charles was talking to the captain and came to tell Dorothy the news.

"The captain tells me this is the steamers last journey carrying train passengers. They're about to open the new Zambezi River Bridge and the railway line will cross the bridge. He's got some bubbly on the foredeck and wants the passengers to have a glass when we go under the bridge!"

"That's interesting," said Dorothy. "History in the making and we're part of it. I'd never have thought we'd be drinking champagne on the Zambezi!"

The huge wooden paddle churned the water as they steamed towards the bridge. It loomed larger as they neared it, a massive suspension bridge spanning the mighty Zambezi. It looked incongruous with its mass of steel and intricate wiring like a monster deposited in the dusty African bush yet a marvellous feat of engineering in such remoteness. Glasses were filled and the steamer's hooters blared as she sailed under the bridge for the last time carrying her regular train passengers. It was the end of an era. The steamer would probably continue carrying local inhabitants and hauling cargo but it's glory days were over.

CHAPTER 8

S alisbury. Southern Rhodesia 1934. They went from hotels to boarding houses for a few months until Charles secured survey work with an electrical company. They moved into a furnished company house and the girls were able to attend another convent, far superior to the hideous education they had had at the Limbe convent. They felt unsettled in their house, wondering and waiting when the next move would come. It did come and Charles was transferred to Gatooma, a small mining and farming town about a hundred miles south of Salisbury.

Dorothy was distraught with the moves and tired of the girls changing schools. Charles was able to finance their education and to Dorothy's pleasure he was actually saving. She hoped it was towards their future.

Charles became friendly with a couple, Harold and Eve Gordon, owners of a gold mine near Gatooma.

"Remember the Gordon's I spoke about?" Charles asked Dorothy. "They've invited us to tea on Saturday."

"Town talk has it they're very wealthy with a very profitable gold mine. I wonder why they want to invite us," said Dorothy, sometimes and understandably suspicious of Charles' activities.

"Actually, he's offered to show me how to find gold. We might strike gold and be able to retire to a life of luxury." Charles wasn't sure whether to act seriously or not.

"Oh for goodness sake Charles. Not again. You're the eternal optimist. Don't waste your time and money on that."

"Nothing ventured, nothing gained. There's no harm in trying," Charles tried to assure her.

Charles and Harold were engaged in conversation at the far end of the veranda for the entire afternoon. Eve was a quiet woman, happy to show Dorothy and the girls the house and garden, almost on a par with the Peterkin's house in Limbe they thought.

"Those two are doing a lot of talking." Dorothy hoped to glean some information from Eve.

"Oh, I'm used to that," laughed Eve. "There's a lot of gold around here and Harold's always willing to part with his knowledge. Some people have been quite successful."

"Is it a costly exercise?"

"It can be, digging the mine, setting it up and so forth. If one's sure there's gold there, it's worthwhile," said Eve casually.

Dorothy didn't like what she heard. If Charles got a bee in his bonnet, nothing would stop him. She'd been there before with him.

Dorothy's and Charles' conversation that night took her back to Hong Kong and Nairobi, a regurgitating nightmare.

"All we have to do is a bit of prospecting and if there's gold there, we'll dig for it. It's quite easy," said Charles.

"What do you mean 'we'? And what's it going to cost to dig the mine? I think it'll be a disaster Charles. Leave it alone, please." There was a tone of despair in her voice.

Charles won the argument and the following Saturday they went prospecting. Dorothy and the three girls loaded the pickup with hammers, picks, sample bags and the all important picnic basket.

"All aboard," bellowed Charles happily.

The girls still loved the back of the pickup even though they were all young teenagers now. Not only were they tomboys, wild little bush pigs, they were very attractive young girls all with blond hair and blue eyes. Charles had a rough map on a piece of paper drawn by Harold. They drove for about ten miles, partly on strip roads then a rough bush road until they reached a rocky outcrop.

It was September and springtime in southern Africa, the warming sap in the msasa trees inciting the green shoots to fabricate a shady canopy over the bush in the shimmering haze, all nature's announcements that the long awaited rainy season was approaching.

"Harold thinks the area south of this kopje might be a good spot." Charles drove off the bush road and the truck rocked over uneven ground and flattened dry bushes, scraping the underbelly and side of the truck. He headed for a big msasa tree and stopped under the spreading branches.

"Will this do?" he asked Dorothy.

"Yes, there's plenty of shade here," she said.

The girls had already jumped off the truck and were climbing a kopje, up the granite rocks and hanging on the trees growing out of the craggy outcrop.

"I often wonder if they were fathered by an orang-utan."

"Me orang-utan," said Charles in a deep voice, thumping his chest with his fists.

"Go on. Go and find your pot of bloody gold." She slapped him on the shoulder. "I'm going to make a fire in those rocks."

Charles put the hammers and picks in a sack and called the girls. They walked about two hundred yards south of the kopje. He showed them what to look for and they spent the next two hours chipping away at likely quartz.

"Tea time." They heard Dorothy's voice in the distance. They left their prospecting tools in situ and headed back to the camp.

"Reminds me of our hut life," said Barbara as she sipped the smoky flavoured tea.

A slice of homemade cake, another cup of tea and they were back to work.

"Some of this looks good," said Charles. "Put them in the sample bags."

It was late afternoon when they left, Charles excited with their find, Dorothy sceptical. He took the samples to Harold the next day and he arranged to send them for analysis.

Three months passed and Charles was still working in Gatooma and spent every weekend at his gold mine. He had employed a gang of workers to help him sink a shaft in the spot where he had prospected with the girls. It had been a lengthy costly exercise. He obtained a mining licence and concession to mine in that area. The timber, equipment and wages had drained his savings.

"Can I say 'I told you so'?" asked Dorothy wearily. "I may as well talk to a brick wall."

"We just haven't come across the seam yet. Indications are it's there. We just have to find it." Charles sounded convincing.

"You keep putting money in to it and you're getting nothing out of it. My advice is – drop it. Drop it before you get any deeper in debt. You've borrowed on the strength of your concession. If you sell everything to Harold, you'll probably break even and get out unscathed."

Charles sat in a big linen-covered floral chair in the sitting room, his stretched out legs crossed at the ankles, his hands clasped behind his head. He grimaced, deep in thought.

"Are you listening Charles?" She could see him weakening under her pressure and she had to maintain it.

"Hmm, I'm thinking." He didn't move for a few minutes.

"Will you think of the girls for once Charles," she hesitated "and me, for that matter."

Charles sighed deeply, lent forward and put his face in his hands. "Alright, you win."

"It's not a matter of winning, you're just being sensible." She was relieved.

"I'll see Harold at the weekend. I know he'll take the equipment off me."

To Dorothy's delight, Charles came out of the mining venture having only singed the tips of his fingers. That was bad enough but she knew how bad it could have been.

They enjoyed nearly twenty months in Gatooma, made some good friends and had social gatherings at the local sports club. The girls had settled at school and picnics in the bush were a regular weekend activity. All was well until Charles had to drop another bombshell on Dorothy and the girls. He was to be transferred yet again, this time to Bulawayo, a town about two hundred miles south of Gatooma.

"I'm tired of all these moves Charles, but it's good to know you're in demand."

"At least it'll be at the end of the school term. Betty finishes this year; Diana has one or two years to do and Barbara a few years yet. There are some very good schools in Bulawayo."

"I hope it'll be our last move." Dorothy sounded tired.

She had no idea what lay ahead.

December 1937. Once again they were on the move. The pickup was packed with suitcases, gardening equipment, kitchen utensils, tins of plant cuttings; everything but the kitchen sink. It was a long journey to Bulawayo on the strip road. The two narrow strips of tarmac mingled with loose stones, dust and occasional potholes. It wound through the bush avoiding rocky outcrops and hills. They would get partly off the strips for oncoming traffic leaving them in clouds of dust. The girls and all their possessions were covered in dust when they arrived in Bulawayo.

Dorothy always felt devastated arriving at furnished company houses. She had her growing family and nothing to show for it. They were never anywhere long enough to put down roots and have their own home. Like their other temporary homes, it was big and rambling. There was electricity but they found a chip geyser at the back of the house that required a fire to heat the water.

They settled well in Bulawayo. It was a big town with a growing population and industrial base. New departmental stores and businesses were springing up in the town centre and it was a hive of activity. Diana and Barbara were in school again. Betty had a flair for art and was gainfully employed as a sign-writer working with window-dressers. It was a friendly town and the girls got to know neighbours and children their own age. Climbing trees became less frequent. They'd bang on an electricity light pole at the junction of the gardens to summons their young neighbours then play cricket or rounders in the gardens.

Dorothy hadn't been well during the year and had paid several visits to the doctor. She had pain in the abdomen and waist and the doctor put it down to her stress and tension over the years and thought it was probably an ulcer. She was a strong woman and put on a brave face and seldom mentioned it to Charles or the girls.

Charles muddled through the year. He was paid well and had

accumulated a little nest egg but was concerned it would never be enough for them to retire on. He wanted the very best for his beloved Dorothy. He knew he had to generate more income and put his ideas to Dorothy. He thought the time was right one Saturday afternoon as they both relaxed on their garden swing.

"I've been giving a lot of thought to a suggestion Harold made when I told him we were moving here."

"Oh?" Dorothy wasn't that interested.

"There are some very successful gold mines around Essexvale and…." He knew she'd interrupt.

"I'm convinced you've got a loose screw."

"Will you just hear me out. I heard the other day that the Mining Department are issuing concessions left right and centre for the area and it's obviously a hot spot. The chap who was telling me says there's an existing mine there and apparently the owner, a chap called Sullivan, wants to sell up due to illness. I checked with the Mines Department and they say it's a viable mine but needs more excavating."

"I really wish you wouldn't do this."

"We've been married for about twenty years now and all we have to show for it is a pile of suitcases and cardboard boxes. I want to be successful for you Dorothy."

Dorothy sighed. "I give up with you Charles."

Charles was excited. He knew that was the green light.

They went to Essexvale the next day to see if they could locate the mine and it's owner. It was a good twenty-mile trip. They drove through the Essexvale Hills, a scenic area of rolling hills and rocky outcrops. The rainy season had started and the bush was green and lush. Essexvale was a very small village of farmers and miners and Charles was able to get directions to Sullivan's mine.

They found an old man loading a truck with a gang of workers. Charles approached him. "Are you Mr Sullivan?"

The man was bent and using a walking stick. "Yes," he said with a croaky voice.

"Hello. My name is Butler. I believe you may be selling your mine?"

"That's right. I can't manage it now. You wanna buy it?"

"Well, I'm considering it."

"I'll show you the assay reports if you like." He limped slowly to a grass hut several yards away before Charles could answer.

They made some sense to Charles having learnt a bit from Harold.

"There's gold down there but needs more digging and I can't do it now." The old man's story confirmed what the Mining Department had told Charles.

They haggled over a price taking into account Sullivan's small loan.

"I want to get this behind me. I'll meet you at the Mining Department tomorrow. There'll be change of ownership forms and a lot of other guff to complete," said the old man and shook Charles' hand.

Charles and Dorothy drove back to Bulawayo. "Signed and sealed," said Charles.

"We forgot to ask him about accommodation. Where's the house?" asked a concerned Dorothy.

"He uses those huts. Didn't you hear him?" asked Charles.

"You must be joking! How can we live in those?" Dorothy couldn't believe it.

"It won't be forever darling. Once we have a good income from the mine, we'll either rent or buy a house. Don't worry!"

"You are such an optimist and now you're chasing your pot of gold. If I asked you, you'd probably tell me it's definitely at the end of the rainbow." Dorothy had a pain in her gut and she wasn't going to argue with him.

Charles was nine months into his mining venture. Betty was working in Bulawayo and was living with a friend. Diana and Barbara had to leave school. Charles put all his savings into the mine and school fees were low on the list of priorities. Dorothy's health deteriorated, she lost weight and her pain continued. She seldom visited the doctor and didn't want to worry the family with her problems.

Their accommodation at the mine was a large square hut used as a sitting room cum office, with a lean-to kitchen off that with a wood stove. Next to that were two rondavals, used as bedrooms. The walls were whitewashed mud with thatched roofs. A small narrow enclosed room made with thatching grass served as the shower. A wooden platform at one end held two ten gallon metal containers complete with hoses. Gravity brought hot water through the hoses and the flow was controlled with plugs at the end of each hose. Their toilet was another separate thatched, roofless hut; a long drop like the Nairobi nightmare.

Diana and Barbara helped Dorothy and Charles with the domestic chores and in the mine. They were back to paraffin lamps and their water was carried from a nearby river in drums slung on a pole between two strong workers. Dorothy went along with the routine yet secretly she hated their existence and knew it wouldn't last long. Charles kept digging but the seams weren't improving. He was finding gold, keeping abreast with the expenses but making very little profit. They realised he was putting in a great deal of effort for little in return.

"This isn't going to work." Charles lay on his bed in their hut, almost thinking aloud.

"You were saving more with the survey work," said Dorothy casually, "and not working so hard."

"I'll advertise it tomorrow and let the Mining Department know it's up for sale. They may know someone who wants to take it further."

Dorothy felt a sense of relief. "Very good idea darling," said Dorothy tactfully. "Do you want to go back to survey work?"

"I'll have to. There's a huge railway expansion going on. There's no shortage of work. Your health concerns me." Charles changed the subject. He rolled over on his bed and looked at Dorothy lying on her bed on the other side of the hut. The wick on the paraffin lamp had burnt down and she was barely visible in the dim light. He got off his bed and turned up the wick on the lamp. "That's better. I've been so bogged down with that damn mine, I hadn't noticed how much weight you've lost." Charles walked over to her, held her head in his hands and kissed her briefly on her lips. "Are you all right?"

"Of course I'm all right. I get a pain now and then in the belly but the doc. says it's probably an ulcer. Don't worry about it." She wanted to be positive.

"Why does he say *probably*? It's either an ulcer or it's not. And why have you lost weight?" Charles was getting concerned.

"Will you stop worrying Charles. Running around the mine, carrying wood, helping with the water from the river and heaven knows what else, is enough for anyone to lose weight."

Charles drove to Bulawayo in the morning and placed an advertisement in the local paper and visited the Mining Department. They assured him they would refer interested parties to him at the mine. He had got to know the chief engineer on the railways, Gordon Robinson, through his survey work with the electricity company and decided to visit him. Charles went straight to his office at the railway headquarters and knocked on his door.

"Well I'm damned. Hello Charles. Come in."

"Hello Gordon. Good to see you again," and Charles held out his hand.

"I understood from Garth you had gone gold panning or something," laughed Gordon.

"Well almost. I bought a mine in Essexvale but it hasn't been that profitable. It needs more money into it but I'm not prepared to take it further," said Charles and got to the point. "I'd like to get back to surveying and wondered if there are any positions on the railways?"

"You must be psychic. We've got an advertisement in tomorrow's paper. Let me give you an application form. You can complete it now if you like, it's pretty straightforward. We'll go through all the applications when they come in but I know how you work and I like you Charles." Gordon didn't beat about the bush.

Charles drove back to Dorothy and the girls at the mine feeling much better and confident. A far cry he thought, from the Nairobi days when he walked the streets looking for employment. He shook his head when he recalled those bad days. "Bloody fool," he said to himself. He was about a mile from the mine when he passed an oncoming car on the narrow dust road. It just passed him when the driver hooted repeatedly. Charles stopped and looked back. The car had stopped; the driver got out and ran back to Charles' pickup.

A man in a suit approached him at the window. "Are you Mr Butler?" The man was out of breath.

"Yes. What's wrong?" Charles thought something had happened at the mine.

"My name is Rabinovitch. I was at the Department of Mines this morning and they told me you may be interested in selling your mine?"

"That's correct." Charles was surprised things had moved so fast and let Rabinovitch take the initiative.

"Do you have the time to show me around now?"

"Yeah, sure." Charles drove on to the mine. He greeted Dorothy and she was about to tell him about Rabinovitch's visit when she saw his car.

"You must have met him on the road?" said Dorothy, "He seems interested in the mine," she whispered as Rabinovitch approached them.

Charles showed him the mine, explaining his unwillingness to put more capital into it. Rabinovitch said he had a few gold mines around the country all of which were managed by his staff. He was primarily an investor.

"I'd like to see the assay reports."

Charles showed Rabinovitch to their square hut. It was dusk and Charles lit the paraffin lamps. They talked for nearly an hour and Dorothy wondered if it was a good or bad sign. They eventually emerged from the hut. Both men seemed happy and Charles showed him to his car. They shook hands in the dark and Rabinovitch's car disappeared into the darkness, dust churning up in the taillights.

"He-he", said Charles, cheerfully rubbing his hands. "I asked him to make me an offer and he offered more than we paid for it! Have we got any bubbly to pop?"

"Would you prefer French? Shall we have a look in the cellar?" joked Dorothy sarcastically. "There might be a bottle of South African wine in the kitchen," said Dorothy excitedly.

"This was all so unexpected and happened so quickly. I've got an advertisement in the paper tomorrow so if people come looking, you can tell them it's sold! I'm meeting Rabinovitch in town tomorrow to finalise everything."

A week later Dorothy, Diana and Barbara were packing up again and moving back to Bulawayo. Dorothy thought she must have cherished Charles with untold love and kept asking herself what other woman would have tolerated such upheaval and squalor in their lives. "Love holds no bounds," she said out loud to herself.

"What did you say Mummy?" asked Diana.

"Oh nothing. Just talking to myself."

The pickup rocked slowly along the dusty road. Diana and

Barbara sat quietly and patiently in the back with the suitcases and cardboard boxes containing their worldly possessions, as they watched the mine and huts become more indistinct amongst the trees. They had become accustomed to this morbid lifestyle. Morbid with their continual moves and no close friends or place to call 'home.' They drifted like a leaf in a gentle breeze not knowing where it will fall.

Charles secured a position with the railways and he worked closely with Gordon Robinson. They had a Dutch gabled house belonging to the railways in the suburbs of Bulawayo. Betty stayed on in the boarding house with her friend. Barbara went to short hand and typing classes and Diana, who wasn't able to type with her little hand, stayed at home with Dorothy and helped in the house. Dorothy continued to be unwell.

"What's wrong Mummy?" Diana was concerned about Dorothy who had spent most of the day sitting on the veranda. "It's not like you to be so quiet. You're always doing things," said Diana sadly.

"I know. I just don't have any energy and I have a bit of pain."

"Where's the pain?" Diana wanted to help. "Do you want to go to the doctor?"

"I don't think he can do anything."

"I think you should go. I want you to get better." Diana hugged Dorothy for a long time, sniffed hard and ran inside.

Dorothy wiped her eyes. She too wondered what was wrong with herself. She had an uncanny feeling when they left the mine; a feeling that it would be her last move, a feeling that a permanent resting place was waiting for her. A sense of peace had enveloped her, peace mixed with sadness.

She pulled herself together and called Diana to help her in the garden. A storm was nearing and Dorothy wanted to cut some roses before the rain ruined them. "Bring me the scissors out of the kitchen will you darling," she called out to Diana.

Diana was delighted Dorothy felt better, helped her cut the roses and took them into the kitchen. They arranged them in two vases and they looked particularly special. Dorothy's pain returned and she had to sit down. Charles arrived home after work and noticed Dorothy wasn't herself.

"Your skin is yellowish my darling. I'm very worried about you and I want you to see the doctor tomorrow."

Charles drove Dorothy to the doctor. She felt too unwell to argue otherwise.

"Come in, Mrs Butler. What have you been up to since I last saw you, please, sit down." Doctor Scott looked at Dorothy's card. "You were last here a year ago."

"I've been feeling very tired recently with a fair amount of pain around here." Dorothy pointed to her upper abdomen.

"Could you lie on the bed please."

Doctor Scott poked and pushed her abdomen for a long time, tapping here, tapping there. "You're quite yellow. I'm sure you have a gall-bladder problem and we probably need to whip that out. I'm referring you to a surgeon and if he agrees, it will be best to go ahead with the operation." Doctor Scott scribbled a letter and sealed it in an envelope. "Will you make an appointment with the sister to see Mr Corrie. I'd like you to see him today."

"Thank you." Dorothy didn't know what to say. The thought of hospital and an operation horrified her.

Charles had waited for her in the car. "What is it?"

"He says it's a gall-bladder problem and wants me to see a surgeon, a Mr Corrie. He's had a cancellation and can see me in half an hour," said Dorothy quietly.

"Well Mrs Butler. You have gallstones and I think we should remove your gallbladder. You won't feel so ill and the pain you're getting is from the stones. I think the sooner we do it the better. Are you happy with that?"

"I'm not happy about any operation but if it's going to relieve the pain, then yes, we must do it."

Dorothy was admitted to the government hospital in Bulawayo three days later. Charles and the three girls accompanied her, devastated that she had to have an operation.

"Now my darlings," Dorothy spoke to her three beautiful daughters. "I don't want you to worry. Betty, Barbara. I want you to carry on with your work and Diana darling, you find yourself a good job. You're very capable and organised."

"Take care of the girls Charles whilst I'm in here."

"We just want you home Mummy," said Barbara.

"You mustn't stay here long. We love you." Diana sat on Dorothy's bed and held her.

"Come on now you lot!" joked Dorothy. "Get yourselves home now and organise your supper." She tried to be their positive strong mother, their mentor, but she felt tired and weak.

Dorothy had her operation the next day. Only Charles visited her in the evening on the advice of the hospital. She was still asleep and Charles thought she still looked a pale yellow. He held her hand by her bedside for a long time, hoping she'd wake but she didn't.

The following afternoon Charles took the girls to the hospital. They walked down the corridor to her ward, hating the smell of disinfectant and mentholated spirit. Dorothy lay motionless her yellow face stark against the white bed linen. The girls look their turn to hold her hand each hoping their touch would waken her.

"Let's all hold her hand together to give her strength," said Diana. They huddled together and grasped Dorothy's thin pale hand. It felt cold. They could feel tears welling up inside but they wanted to stay strong for their mother. Dorothy's eyes flickered and opened and she gazed momentarily at the girls. Her eyes were lifeless, glassy, eyes without a soul. They closed and Dorothy's hand moved briefly in theirs. They rubbed her hand desperate for another sign, something to say she was all right. It never came. It was like a broken umbilical cord, the very core of their life being torn away.

Charles stood on the other side of the bed, speechless. Deep down he felt she had to get better. She was his strength, his reason for living.

A sister came into the room jogging them out of their reeling sorrow. "I think you should let Mrs Butler rest now," she said gently. "Come and see her tomorrow."

"Why isn't she awake and talking to us?" asked Diana.

"Why is she so weak?" came Barbara's question.

"She's had an operation and she needs to rest," answered the sister. "Come now." She encouraged them out of the room. They walked silently through the hospital. Charles saw Mr Corrie at the entrance and stopped to speak to him.

"Just wait in the car girls, I'll be with you in a minute," said Charles. He turned to Mr Corrie. "Hello Mr Corrie. We're very concerned about my wife. She looks very weak."

"Yes," concurred the surgeon. "May I have a word with you?" He led Charles into an empty office off the corridor. "I intended removing your wife's gall bladder yesterday as you know. When we opened her we saw she had very advanced cancer."

Charles covered his face with his hands. "Dear God no." His voice was shaking. "No," he said again.

"I'm very sorry Mr Butler. There was nothing we could do."

"How long? Will she come home?" Charles knew he was asking dreadful questions but he wanted to hear something positive.

"I believe she has only days. I'm very sorry. Would you like someone to drive you home?" Mr Corrie seemed concerned.

"No," said Charles. "No. Thank you. I'll be all right." He walked out of the hospital and to the waiting girls, all squashed into the cab of the pickup, no time for fun in the back. Charles broke the news to them as they drove back to the house.

The phone rang at the house at seven o'clock the next morning. Charles' heart sank. It was the hospital and they wanted them to go there right away. They walked silently along the corridor to Dorothy's room and the sister was waiting for them.

She had to tell them the news. "I'm sorry, Mrs Butler died a short while ago."

The girls shrieked and burst into tears. They looked at Charles, his face covered with his hands. They held out their arms to each other and they hugged each other for support. The sister waited a few minutes. "We've prepared her and you might like to see her."

"Oh Mummy," said Betty. They continued to hold onto each other.

"Come my darlings." Charles seemed to draw inner strength and for a fleeting moment he believed it was Dorothy, watching them in the passage. The sister opened the ward door and they filed in, in ritual crocodile formation, the unwritten law of seniority falling into place as it did so many times before on the dusty footpaths in their adored bush. This time Dorothy was well ahead of them, waiting. They stood at the foot of the bed, grasping one another. They found it hard to look at Dorothy. Only her face was visible above the white linen bedcover, her eyes closed. The sisters had put little pink rosebuds around her head.

Barbara spoke first. "Mummy would hate those rosebuds."

"They're just not Mummy," added Diana.

There was an air of frivolity in their statements, mitigating the gravity of the moment and cognizant of veiling the profound reality before them.

Charles kissed Dorothy on the lips and held his head against hers for a moment, tears in his eyes. He beckoned the girls and the line of seniority followed once more. The sister was standing quietly in the corner of the room. "Can I take you for a cup of tea?" They left the room in silence, not looking back as though being guided to go forward now with their lives.

Lightning Source UK Ltd.
Milton Keynes UK
UKHW021305071222
413541UK00023B/741